Praise f... Kumashiro...

"This b... ...cher educators, and ad... involved in advocating ...ation."

—Grace Lee Boggs, The Boggs Center

"The education reform movement has taken a page from the playbook of the gaming industry to ensure that children of color and poor children are highly represented among the losers! Kumashiro is a remarkable sleuth who guides us through the tangled web of ideology, venture philanthropy, and political chicanery as he shows us how the deck is stacked, how the game is played, who gains, and who loses. Join him in a clarion call to build a movement to reclaim public education, to save our children from becoming serfs in the Information Age, and our democracy from becoming a relic of the past."

—**Robert P. Moses**, The Algebra Project

"Both eminently reasonable in his arguments and passionate in his defense of public school teachers caught in the crosshairs of the current educational reform movement, Kevin Kumashiro unveils how corporate interests, an undue reliance on non-research, and conventional 'common sense' remedies are in fact scape-goating teachers and exacerbating educational inequality. Courageous, blunt, and hopeful, *Bad Teacher!* offers a democratic vision for true educational change."

—**Sonia Nieto**, University of Massachusetts at Amherst

"This book comes at a critical time. Kumashiro provides us with an engaging and insightful analysis of what's wrong with the current direction being taken to reform public education. He also offers wise and practical ideas on how we might go about improving the nation's schools. Anyone seeking to understand why so many of the reforms we have pursued have failed will benefit from reading this book."

—**Pedro A. Noguera**, New York University

"*Bad Teacher!* is a provocative effort to reframe the current debate about school reform. Kumashiro explains why we should think differently about the prescriptions that are now taken for granted—and wrong."

–**Diane Ravitch**, New York University,
author of *The Death and Life of the Great American School System:
How Testing and Choice Are Undermining Education*

"Unlike any other time in history, public education and teachers in particular are being blamed for our nation's shortcomings. In *Bad Teacher!* Kevin Kumashiro expertly examines the many forces working against public education, and how and why these forces are at play. In so doing, he lends hope that there is a better way forward for the American education system."

–**Dennis Van Roekel**,
President, National Education Association

"*Bad Teacher!* is oh-so-smart and timely. After decades of calculated disinvestment, our public schools are in terrible crisis. This book attacks head-on the ragged patchwork of 'school reform' that has left us without even the vocabulary to frame what's gone wrong. Stuck in the binarisms of 'winners and losers,' 'achievers and the undeserving,' we have lurched from thoughtless intervention to madcap experimentation to (ad)venture capital tossed about as hysterically as confetti at a funeral. Against the backdrop of such tragic incoherence, Professsor Kevin Kumashiro's smart, quiet, lucid study cuts directly through the noise. With both empiricism and empathy, he wrestles our attention back to the needs of America's youth—the children whose collective education foretells our destiny as citizens."

–**Patricia J. Williams**, Columbia Law School

The Teaching for Social Justice Series

William Ayers—Series Editor
Therese Quinn—Associate Series Editor

Bad Teacher!

How Blaming Teachers Distorts the Bigger Picture

Kevin K. Kumashiro

Foreword by William Ayers and Therese Quinn

Teachers College, Columbia University
New York and London

Published by Teachers College Press, 1234 Amsterdam Avenue, New York, NY
10027

Library of Congress Cataloging-in-Publication Data

Kumashiro, Kevin K., 1970–
Bad teacher! : how blaming teachers distorts the bigger picture / Kevin K.
   Kumashiro ; Foreword by William Ayers and Therese Quinn.
      pages cm. — (The teaching for social justice series)
   Includes bibliographical references and index.
   ISBN 978-0-8077-5321-7 (pbk. : alk. paper)
      1. Educational change—United States. 2. Teaching—United States. 3. Public
   schools—United States. I. Title.
   LA217.2.K86 2012
   371.102—dc23   2011045597

ISBN 978-0-8077-5321-7 (paperback)

Printed on acid-free paper
Manufactured in the United States of America

19   18   17   16   15   14   13   12   8   7   6   5   4   3   2   1

To my mom

Sherrie Lou Kumashiro

who teaches me still

Contents

Foreword

Bad teacher!

The phrase echoes through the culture at speed, the ready response to a thousand questions: Why don't our kids know any history or geography? Why do they compare poorly in international competitions? Why can't Johnny read or Sally spell? Why is there an epidemic of childhood obesity? There's a simple answer, and everyone knows it: Bad teachers!

The rhythm of it sounds like the scolding of a dog that's just misbehaved: the exaggerated frown of the master, the forced eye-to-eye contact, and the reproachful finger wagged threateningly in the face of the accused. Bad teacher!

Kevin Kumashiro deconstructs the "bad teacher" stereotype here with grace and force, showing it to be in effect a mighty metaphor and a deeply dishonest narrative in the service of a specific ideology. By shining an oversized spotlight on a minor problem, and scapegoating people who are in fact an essential part of the solution, accountability is sidestepped and responsibility shunned.

Still, "bad teacher" is a handy cliché, pithy, memorable, broad and vague enough to drive an entire fleet of yellow school buses through. It's a frame that's air-tight: whenever a politician says, for example, "We need to get the lazy, incompetent teachers out of the classroom," we all feel ourselves nodding dully; we don't jump up and say, "No, please leave the lazy, incompetent ones there for our children and grandchildren." The politician's shaping of the issue and naming of the problem cries out for a single answer. Fire the bad teachers!

Let's say we did fire all the bad teachers, however defined or described. What then? Did classes suddenly become smaller, schools better-resourced? Is outdoor playtime in place and obesity a thing of the past? Are kids now focused and engaged? Is poverty eliminated and health insurance available to them? Are guns and drugs out of their communities, and their local libraries open every day?

The "bad teacher" stereotype is a construction that completely misses the mark as diagnostic tool or call-to-action. There are of course—in a profession of millions—folks who are uninspired and uninspiring, weak and ineffective, individuals who are not up to the challenges and demands of this highly intellectual and ethical work, and just plain wrong for the job. But overwhelmingly people who choose teaching as a calling are dedicated, hard-working, and committed, willing to take up this backbreaking and mind-crunching assignment as an act of love and service.

One counterpoint would be to ask a different set of questions: what makes a good teacher; what qualities constitute goodness in teaching; what policies would promote the good? Perhaps rather than an exclusive and anemic focus on the "bad," we should invest resources, intellectual effort, and energy on promoting and supporting the good.

Today's controlling metaphor is schools-as-businesses, with students as the raw material bumping along the assembly line while test-prep information is stuffed into their little up-turned heads by low-paid clerks disguised as teachers. Within this model it's rather easy to think that privatizing a space that was once public is a natural event; that standardized state-administered (but privately developed and quite profitable) tests is a rational proxy for learning; and that a range of sanctions on students, teachers, and schools—but never on lawmakers, foundations, corporations, or high officials—is logical and level-headed.

This is the new school-reform norm, promoted by a band of dilettante billionaires who work relentlessly to take up all the available space, preaching, persuading, and promoting, always spreading around massive amounts of cash to underline their fundamental points: dismantle public schools in favor of some sort of privately-controlled administration; destroy the ability of teachers to speak with any sustained or unified voice and crush the unions; sort the winners from the losers through a relentless regime of test and punish.

Kevin Kumashiro offers a dazzling rebuttal to all of this. He values teaching as knotty, complicated work requiring patience, wonder, sustained focus, intelligent judgment, an open heart, and an inquiring mind. He understands that we need good teachers to both practice and promote the core values of a free people: initiative and courage, creativity and imagination. And for this we need a society that embraces and supports teachers whole-heartedly and without reservation.

William Ayers
Therese Quinn

Acknowledgments

A great big hug is but a small token of my deep appreciation to the many people who supported me in writing this book.

To Bill Ayers, Erica Meiners, and Ann Schulte, for the brilliant, generous, helpful, invaluable feedback, questions, critiques, suggestions, and mentorship.

To my writing group, Alice Kim, Therese Quinn, Eve Ewing, and Erica and Bill, for inspiring me to continue writing creatively.

To Candice Dawson and Kay Fujiyoshi, my advisees and research assistants, for the expansive background research and editorial support.

To Carole Saltz, Jean Ward, Emily Renwick, and all of the amazing staff at Teachers College Press whose work pre-, in, and post-production made this book possible, including the anonymous reviewers whose encouragement and suggestions strengthened this book.

To the various publishers who gave permission to reprint previous writings.

To the many educators, activists, researchers, colleagues, and loved ones, including those whom I am forgetting to mention here or of whom I am not even aware, who paved the way for this book. In solidarity and with hope.

Have I Got a Story for You!

One night, just as I started writing this book, several friends came to my home for a potluck dinner and "game night." The first game was a get-to-know-you activity that erupted with jokes and laughter and revelations, but it was the second game, a competitive board game that we played twice, which was most memorable for me. It had been years since I had played board games with friends, and yes, I loved it. I loved reliving what it feels like to win. Twice.

The neighbors of my childhood home surely knew that I loved winning because my brothers and I often yelled at each other as loudly as possible whenever we disagreed on who won, and the presence of guests did not stop us. We saw that winning came with extra rewards that often exceeded the applause that follows board games, such as praise, attention, admiration, and other lingering responses that boosted our self-esteem. In high school I competed every year in music and submitted extra credit in classes whenever possible, placing faith in the value of such musical and academic awards for confirming my talent, smarts, and promise. Earlier, I insisted on joining the neighborhood baseball team, imagining the boost to my popularity when I had been worrying so much about not being boyish enough. Even when I was very young, I remember racing my brothers and sister to sip from my uncle's cans of beer, bringing me and my red face attention and laughs from my older relatives. And in contrast, losing came with criticism, or disapproval, or simply silence, and who wants that? We can all benefit from constructive criticism and character building, but I, for one, would not choose to lose all the time or to face ongoing criticism and disapproval.

For me, winning meant being better than others. That was how I began to define who I was and what I was to do, and in deciding which interests to pursue, I followed those that led me to stand out and quit those that did not. One year while in elementary school, I could not stop talking about wanting to play baseball, so my parents finally signed me up, but I quickly concluded that one of the coaches was extra harsh on those of us who were not the stars, so after several weeks, I quit. I loved logic puzzles and math games, so in middle school I tried a few math competitions, but they were too difficult and I was constantly eliminated early on, so I quit. As I became an adult, I remember asking my mother whether she was concerned that I started and quit so many things while growing up. My mother did not seem concerned. Like my siblings, I was just trying to figure out what I wanted to do, and what I wanted to do was not merely that at which I was good, but that at which I was the best, like at the trombone, which I played throughout middle and high schools, winning awards and even becoming my high school marching band's drum major. I needed to feel like I was the best.

As a teenager, my choices seemed like common sense to me. Of course I would choose winning over losing, if those were the only options, and especially if I already saw that I could win. And perhaps that is the power of common sense, to make me believe that I always have such choices, that I can choose whether or not to play, without realizing that there just might be other possible ways of playing any game. What if the math gatherings consisted of finding a partner and coming up with a solution that neither of us could have come up with alone, rather than to compete? What if the music gatherings involved teaching one another a song that exceeded what any of us already knew, rather than to compete?

I have become so conditioned to want to win that I often forget that there are always other possible ways of playing. Games do not always have to produce losers. And certainly when it comes to children, society should be asking whether it really wants any of them to lose. Politicians and pundits today seem to be unable to talk about educational reform in terms other than competitions, such as being the best in the world or racing to the top, in which only some can win while all others must lose. Even reforms that seem to say that everyone can win are nonetheless creating winners and losers, such as No Child Left Behind's mandate of 100% proficiency in reading and mathematics by 2014—a rate that has never been reached by any nation in the world—which actually sets many up to lose because of the sanctions that follow when failing to meet that unattainable standard. School reform is making the failures of vast numbers of America's children inevitable. What is going on?

WINNERS AND LOSERS

Lani Guinier[1] tells the story of a children's party in which girls competed against boys to carry a golfball in a spoon in a relay race across the yard. The girls won, and in a rematch, won again. Sitting on the sidelines were the parents and older relatives who were analyzing the game. Why did the girls keep winning? What was it about the boys that prevented them from winning? What could the boys do differently to win? Until one of the children's grandmothers shifted the analysis by asking, "Who designed the game?"

In a competition, there are many ways to make sense of success and failure, and of winners and losers. The relay race can be seen as a metaphor of inequity and power differences in broader society, and the adults' analysis of the race, a reflection of the common ways that people observe and understand how inequity and power operate. When making sense of a competition or conflict, Guinier suggests that there are at least three types of questions that we should be asking, reflecting three ways of understanding power and powerlessness.

We tend to ask only the first question, *Who is winning and who is losing?* This is perhaps the most common way of analyzing a competition or conflict, as it tries to make sense of how the winners are able to overpower the losers in an overt struggle. The initial questions of the adult observers of the golfball relay race illustrate this; people often have the intent of trying to solve the problem by fixing the losers by helping them to compete better.

But as represented by the grandmother's question, struggles are not always overt. Struggles can be covert when they have already erased other possible ways of relating, engaging, and competing. In other words, inequity and power differences can result not simply from one group overpowering another in a competition, but also from one group defining or in other ways indirectly manipulating the very rules of that competition in ways that advantage them. Not even debated are alternative ways of competing, or what counts as playing or winning. Therefore, the second type of question to ask when analyzing inequity and power is, *Who made the rules?* The girls were the ones who chose the golfball relay race as the game to play. This is not to say that girls are inherently better coordinated, but it is to say that they likely chose a game in which, knowingly or not, they would prevail.

The boys knew that they were losing. They knew that the girls designed the game. Yet they persisted in playing and even demanded a rematch, reflecting an unspoken set of assumptions that the game was fair, that they could still win, and therefore that playing was something that they should want to do. They were making the choice to play, they were giving their consent to the rules and value of the game, without even realizing that they were doing so, which leads to the third type of question to ask: *What is the story that we tell the losers to get them to want to continue playing?* Beyond overt and covert struggles are latent ones—that is, struggles that involve shaping another's consciousness in ways that gain their consent to engaging in something contrary to their own interests, but without their knowing that this is happening. Certain stories can convince the less powerful to cooperate, to abide by the rules, and to continue playing the game. This is precisely what is happening today with public education.

PROBLEMS AND SOLUTIONS

We hear about winners and losers in education all the time, from nations that outperform the United States on standardized test scores to states winning millions in a Race to the Top. One of the most common ways of defining problems in education is with the "achievement gap," or the gap in standardized test scores between, on the one hand, White American and Asian American students, and on the other, all other students of color, including Black, Latina/o, Native American, and Pacific Islander students. Most commonly the question being asked is, *Who is winning and who is losing?* That is, who is doing well on standardized tests and who is lagging behind? The answers to such questions lead to all sorts of calls for programs and resources to "close the gap," to raise the scores of those students being left behind by preparing them to better answer the test questions.

Less commonly asked is *who made the rules* to this system of testing? And more specifically, are tests constructed in ways that advantage those groups that are already scoring well? Standardized, norm-referenced tests show where any given student ranks in comparison to other students who took the same test—that is, how they compare or refer to the majority or norm. This means that there will always be some students scoring low, some scoring high, and many scoring in the middle. One common argument about the value of such tests is that they are more objective, compared to grades that can be inflated or rankings within a less competitive subset of students. But such tests are not objective.

Choices have to be made about what types of questions to include on such tests, and one criterion for making those decisions is how those who previously took such tests scored on those questions. What this looks like in practice is the existence of several questions on the test that do not count toward a student's score and, instead, are potential questions for future tests that are evaluated in terms of how the group of test takers as a whole answer them. If those questions are not correctly answered by the students who are doing well on the tests, then they are not retained as future test questions, thereby ensuring that the test produces a distribution of scores that mirrors the current distribution. There exist all sorts of questions that could be asked, including questions that reflect different cultural referents and different learning styles, as well as different ways of answering questions, but only certain questions and answers count, resulting in a testing process that works to advantage those groups who are already doing well.

A range of other criticisms has long been voiced about the reliance on standardized tests as the sole or even primary indicator of student learning and progress. Such criticisms include cultural biases in question content and answer evaluation; the lack of alignment between test content and curriculum standards, as well as the larger disconnect of emphasizing norm-referenced assessments in a context that supposedly values standards-based instruction and that, therefore, should emphasize standards-referenced assessments;

the lack of standardization and oversight of scoring the open-ended portions of tests; and the narrowing of curriculum that results when placing high stakes on test performance, including the reduction or elimination of other subject areas in order to focus on basic reading and mathematics.

Yet even critics who argue that standardized testing is not a effective measure of student learning can be found saying the opposite, such as when arguing that other reform initiatives like multicultural curriculum or student-centered instruction have proven to be successful in improving education, and then point to the high test scores of this school's program or that country's school system as evidence. In other words, even those who are critical of standardized tests are sometimes reinforcing the underlying story that standardized tests effectively and accurately measure learning. Therefore, rarely asked but essential for analysis is the third type of question, *What is the story that we tell the losers to get them to want to continue playing?* How are we talking about and framing the concept of testing to get those who do not do well, and even those who are critical, to continue placing value on standardized tests?

The practice of standardized testing has been framed in such as a way as to make it seem fair, effective, objective, and incontrovertible. Changing how we assess learning requires not merely changing the tests; it requires changing how we think about tests and testing.

As long as educational improvement means higher test scores, three assumptions remain unchallenged: Standardized tests effectively measure all students' learning, learning means doing well on those tests, and teaching means raising those scores. These three assumptions then lead to policy directives, such as requiring that tests come with rewards for doing well and sanctions for not. Students scoring well should receive recognition, and students scoring poorly should not be promoted or graduated. Teachers who appear to raise their students' scores should receive merit pay, and teachers who do not should be more regulated in what and how they teach, or fired. Schools that meet average yearly progress (AYP) should be publicly praised, and schools that do not should be "turned around" by firing those responsible for this failure, namely, all the staff. And in the face of failure, parents should have options to choose from charter and other schools for their children. These were precisely the requirements for states to be eligible for the $4.4 billion in the first two rounds of federal Race to the Top funds in 2010–11, in which states competed for large block grants to improve public education.

This reliance on standardized tests as the sole or even primary gauge of student learning, teacher efficacy, and school quality is problematic for several reasons. First, as described earlier in this Introduction, because of limited content and inconsistency in scoring, the tests themselves do not tell us much.

Second, the problems in public education are much bigger than the gaps in test scores. Gloria Ladson-Billings[2] has argued that our nation's preoccupation with test scores masks more structural and systemic problems with public education. She uses the federal budget as a metaphor. In any given year, the federal government struggles to balance its budget and to avoid a budget deficit where the amount spent exceeds its income. Over time, these deficits add up to a national debt, which over the past century, and especially the past few years, has increased to its current level of over $14 trillion. Financed by government borrowing, this debt requires hundreds of billions in interest each year, which helps to explain why, even in those years that the United States has had a balanced budget, the national debt continued to grow. Heated public debates between political parties over "pork" spending that prevents a balanced budget mask the larger problem of the steadily increasing national debt. Annual budget deficits, in other words, are merely part of a much larger problem.

So, too, with the achievement gap, which is part of a much larger problem of what Ladson-Billings calls the "education debt." From its history of segregating students by race to its current system of inequitable funding between communities, the educational system has worked to disadvantage certain groups, making the achievement gap inevitable. Merely raising test scores does not solve the larger problem, and instead serves as a distraction that allows the underlying inequities to persist.

Third, the gaps in test scores are being used to justify initiatives that exacerbate inequities. When schools do not meet AYP, they must divert a significant amount of time and resources away from teaching in order to meet new requirements, including increased reporting requirements. Teachers also change their teaching, devoting more time to testing and test preparation, which often involves narrowing and refocusing the curriculum with the hopes of preparing students for success on basic reading and mathematics tests. What results is a lower percentage of teachers' time focused on teaching, and a lower percentage of class time focused on a rich and encompassing curriculum, despite the compelling evidence that students more effectively learn basic literacy and numeracy when such subjects are integrated across the disciplines. That is, students learn more with a broad and challenging curriculum that is developed by their teachers, not a narrowed one that is scripted and standardized across contexts.

Under current reforms, the more students struggle, the less their schools are allowed to teach, and the less they are made to look like flourishing school systems in this country and to other nations. In other words, current reforms are making even more substantial the differences between schools for the elite and schools for all others. So, too, is the case with district-level reforms. Urban districts with high poverty and large populations of students of color are much more likely to have mayoral control of schools and appointed school boards, hundreds of millions of dollars of investments by venture philanthropies that are experimenting with such reform initiatives as charter school programs and fast-track alternative teacher certification programs. This happens despite the lack of research that shows that any of these changes actually improves education. Reforms are creating two tracks for students, but such outcomes are not often apparent in discussions about education.

HEROES AND VILLAINS

Language has the power to mask certain realities or to de-historicize certain concepts. Today, for example, a range of competing proposals exist on how to reform public schools, and yet, in the media, in policy papers, and in speeches by politicians, only certain initiatives seem to count as reform, and only certain actors as reformers. All other actors are cast as defenders of the status quo, even those who are advocating for fundamental change. Perhaps best illustrated by the 2010 film documentary *Waiting for "Superman,"* "reform" means that students must be focused exclusively on scoring well on standardized tests, teachers must be held accountable to raising those test scores, and parents must be given the choice to move their children out of failing schools, especially when teacher unions are believed to be working tirelessly to protect the bad ones.

In this characterization, all of education rests on the shoulders of teachers, hence the frequency of blaming teachers for all that is wrong with some public schools, and of praising reformers—like former chancellor of DC public schools Michelle Rhee—who have the fortitude to fire the lazy and incompetent ones who predominate. This praise and blame come from even our highest leaders. Soon after taking office, President Barack Obama urged, "It's time to start rewarding good teachers, stop making excuses for bad ones."[3] No more excuses. More recently in the summer of 2010, Secretary of Education Arne Duncan gave a speech in which he proclaimed, "The biggest single thing we can do is get great teachers into these struggling schools."[4]

Of course, not all is bad. Some Americans are quite satisfied with the public schools that their children attend, because some public schools are well resourced, prestigious, and successful at educating children. In fact, according to the 2011 Phi Delta Kappa (PDK)/Gallup poll, over 70% of Americans said that they have trust and confidence in the men and women who are teaching children in the public schools.[5] But the dialogue on public education tends to focus on the schools for other people's children, which are typically schools that serve large percentages of students of color and students living in poverty, and it is these schools that are characterized as failing, as needing to be turned around, and exemplary of all that is wrong. And such a characterization gives justification for an all-out assault on public education, and a call for sweeping changes.

These sentiments help to explain why alternative routes to becoming teachers have gained widespread support. Clearly, there are villains in this story—those groups who are contributing to the problem. This includes teacher unions that are making excuses for and protecting bad teachers and university-based teacher preparation programs that are producing mediocre teachers in the first place. The heroes are those who stand in contrast, like the superintendent who fires a bunch of principals and teachers, the elected official who pushes legislation that weakens unions, and the program that offers faster routes to becoming teachers by removing barriers that, for too long, have prevented the best and brightest from becoming teachers.

Adding to the heroism of some reformers is the appropriation of the language of "civil rights." Programs like Teach for America, for example, claim to be challenging the established institutions, the defenders of the status quo, in order to better serve the neediest of children, and therefore signal "the new civil rights movement" in this country, according to the book by Teach for America founder and CEO Wendy Kopp.[6] Kopp frames Teach for America in the tradition of the civil rights activism of the 1950s and 1960s, which is ironic because Teach for America is deeply connected to organizations with a long history of actually challenging the gains of the Civil Rights Movement (which will be described in Chapter 4).

A further irony is the image often associated with Teach for America, namely, the U.S. Peace Corps. Kopp claims that Teach for America was inspired by the Peace Corps and is structured similarly to appeal to the young idealists who postpone their professional careers for a couple of years to help a group of people different than themselves who are in need. I was one of those idealists who joined the Peace Corps right after college, but soon after I began, I learned from my colleagues about a lesser known history to our volunteerism. The Peace Corps was founded during the Civil Rights Movement in 1961. It not only offered young adults an option out of military service in a time of war, but also offered the nation a way to show that its foreign interests were altruistic and not imperialist, as critics of U.S. involvement in the Vietnam War were claiming. Yet the Peace Corps functioned to spread American ideas and interests to developing nations, serving a key role of exporting and valorizing capitalist ideology during the Cold War, which means that volunteers, knowingly or not, were contributing to a colonizing, assimilating mission of the Peace Corps.

The parallel, here, with the colonizing, assimilating mission of public schooling in the United States is uncanny. In the 19th-century United States, the recruiting of young, unmarried, White women into teaching echoed the ideology about White women teachers that pervaded imperial Britain, in which their role was to educate not only the White working class but also the Native people and people of color who were colonized by Britain or the United States.[7] Public schooling, as embodied in the White woman teacher, played a central role in assimilating racially and culturally diverse groups throughout the history of U.S. national growth, both its physical growth with Westward expansion and its demographic growth with increased immigration and forced incorporation via the conquest of native groups and enslavement of Africans. White women teachers even today symbolize the goal of public schooling to assimilate difference, all couched in the image of nurturing and care, as depicted in popular Hollywood films like *Dangerous Minds* and *Freedom Writers,* where young White women teachers lift up their poor students of color. The metaphor of teacher-as-savior has a long history in American schools, and Teach for America capitalizes on this image.

In contrast, this is not to say that "traditional," university-based teacher education is the vanguard of civil rights. It is not. The recent debate and controversy over whether to include or remove language regarding diversity and social justice in the professional standards of the National Council for the Accreditation of Teacher Education (NCATE) reveals that teacher education, as a profession, is itself struggling over where it positions itself in terms of civil rights. But my point, here, is that language has the power to influence public opinion, and the appropriation of such concepts as "reform" and "civil rights" has certainly changed the conversation about public schooling today. The common sense of educational reform not only misplaces the blame and obscures the bigger picture, but also embraces reforms that make the problems even worse.

With "reformers" like Michelle Rhee and Arne Duncan, billionaire funders that are leveraging their wealth to change the preparation and evaluation of teachers, and trend-setting legislation in early 2011 that weakened collective-bargaining rights in Wisconsin, Indiana, Ohio, Illinois, and elsewhere, a new common sense has emerged about what it means to reform public education, and the target is clear: teachers. The need to see the bigger picture and reframe the debate is profoundly urgent.

This book examines current educational reforms in the United States, with particular emphasis on how the language used to talk about such reforms masks the bigger picture. Chapter 1 describes the commonsensical ideas that permeate public perceptions about school reform and the role of the teacher. Chapter 2 illustrates the power of framing to influence public opinion, and highlights four prevailing frames about school reform: fear, values, standards, and competition. Chapter 3 turns specifically to teacher preparation, and examines initiatives to redefine teacher quality and preparedness. Chapter 4 follows the money by tracing the role of philanthropy and corporations in shaping educational reform, with particular attention to examples in Chicago. The Conclusion offers suggestions for reframing the debate about educational reform and reclaiming public education, including an advocacy framework for engaging in multiple strategies to bring about change.

The assault on public education is both daunting and demoralizing. The bigger picture can seem overwhelming at times. But seeing the bigger picture also reveals opportunities to intervene, collectivize, and transform. There is much reason for hope in reclaiming and rebuilding public education.

CHAPTER 1

Common Sense About Educational Reform

In my early 20s, I headed to Nepal to begin work as a volunteer with the U.S. Peace Corps, and I quickly learned that I did not have much common sense there. In the village where I was stationed, there were many aspects of schooling that my neighbors seemed to take for granted as the ways schools are and should be, but that did not align with my own assumptions about schooling. For example, I wanted to seat students in mixed-gender groups but learned that boys always sit together on one side of the room and girls on the other because the large numbers of students squeezed onto small benches made physical contact inevitable, which was fine among students of the same gender but culturally inappropriate otherwise. I tried to manage the classroom with dialogue and verbal admonitions but was often told by teachers and students alike that controlling the classroom meant hitting those who misbehaved. I risked being seen as lacking authority because I did not carry a stick.

Perhaps most significant, I wanted to introduce activities, materials, and sample problems that I had created on my own, but was told that class lessons had always consisted of what was in the official textbooks, issued by the government, common to all schools, and the basis for the annual tests that determined whether students would move to the next grade level. Common sense dictated that teachers were to go over the solutions to the problems, which students were to copy down and memorize, primarily because the high-stakes exams consisted of these very problems. By not doing what was expected, and by presumably jeopardizing their chances of passing the exams, I was confronted with criticism by students who complained not merely that I was not teaching well, but that I was not teaching at all. What I was doing did not make sense to them.

My initial reaction was to view Nepali schooling disparagingly, as inferior to my own American upbringing. But further reflection forced me to turn that critical lens onto my own assumptions about American superiority and exceptionalism. What are aspects of American education that I have been presuming to be how schools have always looked here at home and, perhaps more important, how schools should be made to look everywhere else?

As is the case in Nepal, many aspects of schooling in the United States have become so routine and commonplace that they go unquestioned. Across the nation and for both young children and adolescents, schools generally open from early morning until mid-afternoon, Monday through Friday, from the end of summer until the beginning of the next summer. Students spend most of their time studying the four "core disciplines" of reading, mathematics, social studies, and the natural sciences, and less frequently, foreign languages, the arts, physical education, and vocational education. Classes in each subject generally last between 1 and 2 hours, meet every day or every other day, and consist of one teacher, perhaps an adult assistant, and a group of about 10, 20, 30, maybe 40 students. Students are usually grouped by age, sometimes by gender, and often by some measure of ability. Teaching and learning usually take place in a four-walled room where students sit for most of the period, working out of shared books or writing on shared topics or engaging in shared experiments. Teachers are expected to know more than the students, determine what students are supposed to learn, structure the class in such a way that students learn what they are supposed to learn, and then assess whether they learned it with exams or assignments. Students are expected to follow instructions, work hard, and do homework in order to learn what they are supposed to, and the grade, score, or rank with which they end is meant to reflect the degree to which they succeeded. Framed as common sense in education, this is what many people take to be what "real" schools look like.

Throughout history, schools have taken on a variety of forms, and even today, some schools design alternative ways to schedule classes, organize the curriculum, and group students, such as with block scheduling, interdisciplinary units, and mixed-age groupings, as well as alternative types of activities, assessments, and goals, including field-based projects, portfolio assessments, and cooperative learning. Yet over the past century, the commonsensical view of schools has persisted and has hindered attempts to change aspects of schooling that are often taken to be fundamental.[1] Attempts to improve schooling that defy this common sense have been dismissed as biased, as a distraction from the real work of schools, or as inappropriate for children, particularly when the reforms call attention to such hot-button, controversial issues as racism, sexism, poverty, and how these are reinforced in schools.

Common sense narrowly defines what is considered to be consistent with the purposes of schooling. Common sense does not say that this is what schools *could* be doing; it says that this and only this is what schools *should* be doing. Furthermore, as my experiences in Nepal taught me, common sense is not something that just is; it is something that is developed and learned and perpetuated over time. To reform schools, therefore, we must first redefine common sense and reframe how society thinks and talks about education—which begs the question, What is the common sense of education today?

IT'S ALL ABOUT THE TEACHER

FrameWorks Institute is an organization in Washington, DC, that aims to support nonprofit organizations in understanding how the general public understands social issues and strategizing more effective ways to translate research into public dialogue. In 2010, FrameWorks released a study that revealed five primary ways that average Americans make sense of schooling, which parallel the ways that the mass media covers education.[2] This is not to say that everyone in the United States thinks and talks about education in these ways, but it does suggest that certain concepts frequently reappear in public dialogue as common sense.

First, *education means the K–12 classroom*. Generally, people conceptualize education in terms of what teachers are doing in the classroom. In a context where learning is presumed to be measured by standardized tests, this means that improving education is tantamount to improving the ability of the teacher to raise test scores. Much more rare are conversations about education that include other actors, such as support staff, administrators, policy makers, community members, and taxpayers; or other elements of the broader educational system, such as school governance, finance, residential segregation, and health services provision. People do not typically think in terms of a system of education. The media reinforce this narrow perspective with stories of exceptionalism, focusing on individual classrooms and schools, especially with examples of beloved teachers or successful school programs, without connecting to these broader elements.

Second, consequently, the primary actors are those who are most commonly associated with the classroom, which means that *education is what happens between teachers, students, and parents*. Accordingly, even when other elements of the broader educational system, such as funding and resources, are acknowledged as inadequate, learning can happen if teachers, students, and parents simply try hard enough. Reinforcing this perspective are voices in the media from students themselves or adults reflecting on their student years about the quality that they felt was most important to their succeeding, namely, whether their teachers cared enough about them to do what it took to help them succeed. The success or failure of an educational system gets placed on the shoulders of the most visible of individuals in the educational landscape.

Third, *education requires first teaching the basics*. The presumption here is that students cannot learn and are not prepared for their future life outside of school if they have not first learned the most foundational of skills, namely, the "three Rs" of reading, writing, and arithmetic. The basics should come first, which means that all other subjects and skills are secondary, or even distractions. Innovations in curriculum (what we teach) and instruction (how we teach) are often blamed for what is perceived as students learning even less now than students learned in the past. Educational reform, therefore, should return schools to doing what they used to do, and did better, and eliminate or resist the add-ons, the luxuries that we cannot afford right now. The one exception would be the addition of computers, tools that bring the basics into the modern era.

Fourth, *education may be in crisis broadly and in the abstract, but concrete changes are possible if one focuses locally*. The media inundate the American public with stories of failing schools and a crisis of public schools that is both widespread and incredibly complex. This can lead to a sense of being overwhelmed with the size and scope of the problem, and of being helpless to change it. A sense of crisis can lead not to boldness but to cautiousness; not to risk-taking and wide-scale revolution, but to small steps that are perceived to be doable and that have most immediate impact on oneself and one's own children, such as what happens in their classrooms.

In fact, wide-scale educational reform may be opposed precisely because it promises to change how people access resources and benefits, thereby raising questions about whether one's own current level of access will be reduced. Consequently, the fifth common way that Americans make sense of education sums up the first four: *one's responsibility to educational reform is to address the education of one's own child.* The crisis in education is too big for one person to address individually, but that person does have the ability to address what happens in the local classroom, such as by insisting that students learn the basics by teachers who care. When faced with all the problems that exist, that person can at least prioritize the needs of his or her own child. Furthermore, in a context where students are measured against one another, the focus becomes exclusively one's own child, out of fear that the time and resources that a parent or teacher puts into advocating for other students can actually take them away from their role in advocating for their own students. As a result, children, schools, and communities see themselves as competing against one another, and questioning why any parent should advocate or pay or be concerned for anyone else's child.

BAD TEACHER!

The common sense about schools and teachers today does not call on Americans to see the bigger picture, to see a broader system of education. Rather, common sense narrows our vision to the level of the individual. Good teachers make for good schools, and since we hear repeatedly that our schools are bad, so too must be our teachers. At least, some of them.

This reminds me of a recent conversation that I had in one of my classes about the word "bad." I was telling my students that, when I was growing up, "bad" sometimes meant "good," as in, "I really liked that movie, it was *baaaad!*" Words are not transparent and timeless, but can take on different and multiple meanings in different contexts, similar to how "teaching" meant something different when comparing my own professional training in the United States to my students' evaluation of me in Nepal. Furthermore, words have meaning only because there exist other words to compare and contrast. "Bad" only has meaning because there is a contrast, a "good," which is how language in general operates: We understand "dark" only when we also understand "light," or "high" and "low," and so on. In fact, any concept requires that there be others to contrast or relate, which means that we sometimes produce the opposite. We can understand "good" only if we have already defined other things as bad. So, when we create a definition of the good student, consisting of such attributes as high achieving and compliant, we also define entire categories of students as bad, such as the underachieving, the culturally unassimilable, the misbehaving, the impaired, the out-of-the-box thinker, the unique and nonconforming, and so on, and we even try to fix or punish them, as with medication, separation, or signs on their records, in order to uphold a narrow definition of what it means to be good that only few can attain. So, too, with the good and the bad teachers. When we narrowly define the good teacher merely in terms of the ability to raise test scores, we inevitably are categorizing all others as bad, even those who, in so many other ways, are successful, admirable, valuable, impactful, effective, ethical, and good.

There are many possible ways to define the good teacher, but today, we seem to be stuck in a pretty narrow framing.

This should lead us to ask why we think about teachers and education in this way, and from where we got our ideas. Many perspectives exist and are constantly evolving, but only certain perspectives predominate and have come to permeate both official policy and informal conversation. How so? What are the metaphors, the rhetorical strategies, the *frames* being used to influence how the American public thinks and feels and talks about education?

CHAPTER 2

The Power of Framing

I was sitting in my office on the morning of September 11, 2001, when a colleague rushed to my door to tell me that she had just heard that an airplane had crashed into one of the World Trade Center towers in New York City. As the hours passed, more airplanes crashed, both of the towers collapsed, a part of the Pentagon in Washington, DC, was destroyed, and all attention seemed to turn to the terror that had hit U.S. soil. Thousands were presumed to have died, forthcoming tragedies were not ruled out, and the nation seemed paralyzed with grief, fear, and uncertainty. Classes were canceled at the college where I was teaching, so I headed home, glued to the radio and then the television. I wept as I saw many die and heard many witnesses tell their stories of panic and loss. Some of the attackers passed through the airport not far from where I was then living in Maine. I had friends and relatives living in New York City and Washington, DC. I hoped that they were safe. And I hoped that I was safe.

Many people wanted answers. These were not tragic coincidences. These were planned attacks. Why would people want to attack "us"? How could people be so "evil"? Who is responsible? How will we punish "them"? Mixed in with grief, fear, and uncertainty was a profound sense of anger. I remember not being able to eat very much that day. My nausea was but one of the indications that I was, indeed, overcome with sadness and fear. My feelings of sadness and fear resulted not only from acknowledging the attacks on the United States and the deaths left in their wake, but also from anticipating how many in the United States would respond. News commentators were speculating that this was an act of terrorism by Muslim extremists, and political leaders were promising to use all at their disposal to punish those responsible for this "worst act of terrorism on U.S. soil." People wanted revenge. I remember having conversations with my friends in which we feared that, in the name of revenge, many would be unwilling or even unable to recognize the oppressiveness of their own responses. We suspected that many would respond in terribly oppressive ways, and this is exactly what happened.

As U.S. intelligence agencies gathered evidence that "Muslim extremists" were responsible for these attacks, the responses were swift and violent. Abroad, the United States sent more and more military forces to find and punish those responsible. Political leaders called for a war on terrorism that would span not only the Middle East but also the entire globe in an effort to eliminate those who sought to "attack freedom and democracy." Within the United States, more and more individuals seemed to think this war was against anyone who "looked Muslim" or "looked Arab," including those who were misidentified as such because they wore a turban or head covering or simply had darker skin. Such Muslim- or Arab-looking people were treated as potential criminals. They were aggressively scrutinized when trying to board airplanes, and were subject to harassment and abuse. In the months that followed September 11th, the number of reports of hate-related incidences and hate crimes against individuals who looked Muslim or Arab increased dramatically in the United States.

Although political leaders were quick to denounce such racial and religious scapegoating, they themselves were guilty of similar acts of harassment and discrimination. As agencies responsible for fighting terrorism began arresting or harassing many whom they suspected of being connected to the attacks or to future attacks and were denying many of them of their constitutional rights, political leaders were granting more and more powers of surveillance to these agencies to fight terrorism, particularly through the 2001 Patriot Act. In fact, in an eerie parallel to the Japanese American internment during World War II, hundreds upon hundreds of people, including Muslim Americans and Americans of Middle Eastern descent, were rounded up and interned. More and more initiatives were launched to expand the abilities of the government to gather information on how anyone spends their money, what they read in the library or on the Internet, where they travel and when, what they do in their spare time and with whom, and this information could come via neighbors and private companies confidentially. These increased powers may have conflicted with our constitutional and civil rights, but polls indicated that the majority in the United States supported such a compromise.

This was, we were told, a time for the nation to come together. We should stand behind our political leaders and present ourselves as a strong, united nation. We should be proud to be part of the United States and display this pride with flags on our T-shirts and our cars and our desks and our lawns. After all, the United States was said to symbolize freedom and democracy, and to attack the United States was to attack these institutions as well. The pressure to conform to these convictions was significant, as was the penalty for failing to do so. Representative Barbara Lee of California, the sole Congressperson who voiced early dissent for the president's war policies, received death threats. Even in my own neighborhood, news that individuals were being attacked verbally and physically for being "anti-American" prompted a woman and her family to take down a sign from their apartment window that read, "Give peace a chance." Being American required acting in only certain ways and wanting only certain things.

People were afraid, and were kept in a state of fear as the government constantly raised and lowered and raised again the official "terror alert." The media constantly reminded us that the "terrorists" were still out there, planning their next attacks, and although U.S. intelligence was apparently successful in thwarting one attack after another, the "terrorists" continued to evade capture. So long as the enemy was out there, the American public would continue to turn to what it perceived to be a source of strength: strength in our sense of national identity and unity, strength in our president and his ability to fight back.

We later learned that the Bush administration misled the public about the reasons to go to war, and with whom, and where and when. Furthermore, the United States was not as much the innocent victim as the media would have us believe. What some people call terrorist attacks on freedom and democracy can be understood as "blowback." A term first used internally at the U.S. Central Intelligence Agency, "blowback" refers to the unintended consequences of policies and actions abroad that were kept secret from the American public. Many "acts of terrorism" can be understood as blowback from American foreign policies and actions over the past half-century.[1] But such is not often explained, and purposefully so. After all, it might have been the case that the fear we feel is generated in part by those who profit most when we support paying more for greater security, including to contractors and businesses with ties to the Bush administration.

Much can be accomplished when people are afraid. From the financial benefits of business contracts, to the social benefits for the wealthy of a reduced welfare state, to the political benefits for the Bush Administration of increased unity and conformity, there is great profit in the business of fear. Within education, fear similarly drives reform. In fact, fear and a sense of crisis are exactly what bolster the current reforms that would otherwise not be possible.

CAPITALIZING ON FEAR

In the 1980s, the goal of some conservatives to dismantle public education required a "manufactured crisis"—problems framed by misleading data—and for almost 3 decades, the public has been told to fear that the United States is a "nation at risk" of failure.[2] Domestically, a large percentage of students is failing, especially in poorer communities with less resources and presumably—or, some would argue, "consequently"—more crime. Abroad, students from some countries are outperforming American students on standardized tests. Critics argue that students in American schools are failing to learn what is needed to succeed in the workplace and the global market, forcing the nation to devote more of its resources to addressing social ills while compromising its position as a world leader in military strength, scientific achievement, democratic values, and political influence.

If the United States is faltering, and if things were better in the past, as they "traditionally" were, then people are likely to want things to be as they were back then. And if education "back then" was better and is faltering now because of the various "trends" in educational reform like student-centered classrooms, experiential learning, multicultural curriculums, and differentiated instruction and assessment, then people are likely to revert to commonsensical notions of how schools were and should be. People will want to see schools teaching primarily the academic subjects, like the "three Rs" of reading, writing, and arithmetic; or districts implementing standardized curriculums that presumably level the playing field by teaching everyone the same thing; or students scoring well on tests as evidence that they have learned; or teachers using instructional methods that "work" to raise achievement, as categorized by the U.S. Department of Education's "What Works" Clearinghouse. NCLB illustrates such ideas by making explicit what and how teachers are supposed to teach by going back to the "basics," by aligning all lessons to learning standards, by using high-stakes tests to determine student promotion and graduation, and by sticking to scripted curriculums and other instructional methods that are "scientifically proven" to be effective in raising test scores.

The fear over a failing educational system has helped to advance the standards-and-testing movement, which in turn creates opportunities for profit. Scripted curriculums require textbooks, worksheets, teacher guides, and other materials to be purchased by schools or districts. High-stakes tests require testing sheets, scoring services, tutoring services, study guides, and other materials, also to be purchased by schools or districts. Defining only certain methods to be "scientifically proven" privileges certain kinds of research in competitions for funding, publishing, and other forms of support.

Even the delineation of learning standards is profitable, perhaps not financially, but socially and politically. Throughout the 20th century, schools have been critiqued for teaching in ways that reinforce a particular racial, social class, gender, and national consciousness that privileges certain groups and marginalizes others, helping us to understand why the debate over what to include in the standards is a political and highly contested one. By regulating what to teach, the learning standards can privilege certain knowledge, skills, and perspectives, particularly the knowledge, skills, and perspectives of those groups that are defining the standards.

A more recent example of profiting from crisis and fear occurred in the early 2000s, following the devastation of Hurricane Katrina on New Orleans, when the federal government opened the doors to voucher programs (the so-called Katrina Vouchers), which directed public tax dollars to private institutions. Liberal Democrats who had historically opposed school vouchers shifted their position out of fear that they would appear uncaring about those in need. At the same time, neighborhood public schools closed as charter schools opened in their place. The post-Katrina vouchers and charter schools brought about even further inequity, as many impoverished children entered schools with even fewer resources than before. The move toward charter schools has also been fueled by the federal policy to "turn around" failing schools by firing all staff and bringing in new management, including for-profit management companies. Examples of districts in which turnarounds led to the creation of many new charters within the past year include the Chicago, Denver, Detroit, Los Angeles, and Philadelphia school districts, and many of these charter schools outsource their management and other staffing.

Fear makes us less likely to question what has become taken for granted as the solution to our problems, and less likely to seek out a vision of the bigger picture. Fear is what prompts us to seek out reassuring stories that provide a sense of who we are and how we should think. In recent years, particularly in election seasons, one of the most commonly replayed of these reassuring stories was that of the values of the traditional American family.

FAMILY VALUES

In the late 1990s and early 2000s, the Republican Party saw a string of successes at the polls, including the elections of George W. Bush as president and Arnold Schwarzenegger as California governor, and a range of ballot initiatives that undermined human and civil rights across the country,

including changes to law that undermined affirmative action, gay rights, immigration rights, and worker's rights. At
first glance, it may seem difficult to articulate what connected the vast range of issues that Republicans were fighting
for, and similarly, the connective tissue for the issues that
Democrats were fighting for. But across the issues, one theme
or metaphor kept emerging, namely, "family values." This
was perhaps not surprising, given the frequency by which
the media as well as the general public conceptualize and
talk about the nation through the metaphor of family, using
such terms as the "founding fathers," "birth of a nation,"
"sending sons to war," and "daughters of the revolution."
But it does seem surprising that so many issues threatening
the nation's security and well-being, including nuclear proliferation and global warming, paled in comparison to the
visibility given to family values—surprising, that is, until
one recognizes that it was perhaps not the issues that determined how people voted.

Voters are not typically swayed by policy positions;
rather, they vote for what aligns with their identities and
aspirational values, even if it means that they vote against
their own self-interest, economic or otherwise. Successful
candidates, therefore, are not those who run polls and focus
groups to determine the policy issues on which to run their
campaigns, but rather are those who succeed in tapping into
something that lies deeper, at the voter's core sense of self,
particularly their perception of who they are, or who they
would like to be, and what they value. In the George W.
Bush presidential elections in particular, those core values
reflected a particular image of the family.

George Lakoff[3] describes two ways that Americans, con-
sciously or subconsciously, think about the family. The "strict
father" family model is one in which the father is the leader of

the family, knows right from wrong and teaches this to his children, disciplines his children when they go wrong, protects his family from the dangers outside, but does not dote on his children, which would serve as a crutch, and instead expects that they will "pull themselves up by their bootstraps" to make it. Intertwined with this family model are two other values: self-sufficiency, as captured by the rags-to-riches novels of 19th-century American author Horatio Alger, in which young boys escape poverty through hard work; and meritocracy, where those who succeed are those with talent and perseverance. Such values have been echoed in other presidential elections, including stories of both Bill Clinton and Barack Obama rising from humble beginnings.

In contrast is the "nurturant parent" family model, in which parents are more equal in their relationship and in which children are nurtured in their growth rather than disciplined or left to fend for themselves. Many people understand and even identify with both family models, which is why the same person watching various television shows can feel a connection with strict-father families (as in *Father Knows Best*) as well as with nurturant-parent families (as in *The Cosby Show*).

According to Lakoff, what Republicans did was to appropriate the strict-father model and frame their issues metaphorically around the components of this model. For example, like the strict father, the United States is the leader of the world family, and like the father, we know what is right, we do not need to ask others, like the United Nations for permission, and we punish those who go wrong through embargoes or military campaigns. We protect our family from the dangers "outside," be they outside the country, with a strong military and with expensive military equipment, or outside the household, with more prisons and tougher sentencing. And just as fathers do not dote on their children in the strict-father model, the government should not dote on its citizens through social-welfare programs, environmental protection laws, targeted educational funding for disadvantaged communities, and so forth. What at first glance would seem disparate—militarization, incarceration, welfare, the environment, education—become connected to family values, resulting in the perception that, regardless of the issues, the Republican Party or candidate clearly shares "my" values.

It should be noted that, when those values are threatened, voters will be mobilized, as was arguably the case in ballot initiatives and candidate platforms on same-sex marriage. Debates on same-sex marriage raise passion and controversy in American society like few other topics today, perhaps because same-sex marriage challenges the notion that the strict-father family is the only way that a family could or should be.

The ability to frame the debate depends not only on the concept and the language used to convey that concept, but also on the means of communicating that language and on the frequency of that communication. In 2002, Republicans spent four times as much as Democrats on research and got four times as much media time. Conservative leaders, including leaders with ties to the Republican Party, used to hold weekly meetings, led by strategist Grover Norquist, to work out their differences and develop their common messages. Conservative foundations invested heavily in those institutions and projects that could market and sell to the public their policy priorities. Conservatives, including the Republican Party, put vast resources into ensuring that they were framing the debate.

Throughout history, the strict-father family model has been used to regulate the teaching profession in American schools. At times, unmarried women were desirable as teachers because they did not cost much, so long as they left the profession when they got married and fulfilled their duties in the "traditional" family. At other times, unmarried women were undesirable as teachers because, if they were young, they were thought to dote too much on young boys, and if they were older, they were thought to dominate and, in the process, emasculate young boys.[4]

Today this strict-father metaphor has come to frame broader educational reform as well. The standards-and-testing movement that culminated in NCLB is illustrative. Leaders in education should know right from wrong and should prescribe what all students should learn (that is, there should be standards). Students, teachers, and schools should not be given assistance that can function as a crutch but, instead, should be treated equally and held accountable to reach the same standards and demonstrate that they have done so by way of standardized measures (there should be accountability). Schools, teachers, and students should be disciplined when they go wrong and fail to meet standards, as with cuts in funding to schools, loss of autonomy for principals, loss of placements for teachers, and denials of promotion or graduation for students (there should be sanctions). Parents should be able to protect their children from such dangers as lazy peers, unskilled teachers, or immoral school environments, and should have the choice of moving their children to other, better schools (there should be choice).

The four frames of *standards, accountability, sanctions, and choice* become linked together by a metaphor, the strict-father family, which makes the four frames inseparable from one another. The same is true for the frames of family, self-sufficiency, and meritocracy. These strategic framings, in which several frames link inseparably, help us to understand why Democrats who criticize, for example, school choice but continue to use the language of accountability could be seen by some people to be contradictory or simply nonsensical.

FROM STANDARDS TO STANDARDIZATION

Historians are now calling the period from the 1980s through the present the standards-based reform era, signaling the degree to which the frame of standards, and the very narrow way that "standards" is being defined and operationalized, has come to dominate both policy and discourse. This call for standards did not arise in a vacuum. From the Reagan administration's "A Nation at Risk" report that decried the failings of American schools, to the corporate sector's increased interest in shaping public schooling, powerful voices in the 1980s were amplifying the call by some scholars to go "back to basics." Going back to basics involves returning to how some people believe schooling used to be, before the demands of the Civil Rights Movement and the War on Poverty, with these movements' emphasis on the social purposes of schooling, directed schooling toward multicultural curriculum, student-centered pedagogies, and other approaches that embrace diversity. Today's call for curriculum standards, which consists of only certain things, articulated by only certain groups in society, echoes the earlier call for schools to prioritize only certain ways of seeing and living in the world.[5]

Some proponents of curriculum standards claim that the move toward multicultural curriculum made schooling more biased, more partial, and more partisan. But a brief look back in time reveals that schools have always been teaching only certain things from only certain perspectives to only certain groups. For example, both the structure and the curriculum of public schooling have long been critiqued for teaching students a particular racial consciousness that privileges Whiteness and White American culture and identity. In the late 18th century and into the 19th century, common schools (predecessors of public schools) were created for only White students, and as public school systems expanded to include students of color, segregation kept different racial groups apart, with schools for White students receiving far superior resources and prestige. Even when the curriculum content was comparable between schools, the messages were impacting students differently, as Carter G. Woodson argued in *The Mis-Education of the Negro*, which illuminated ways that Eurocentric curriculum taught Black students subservience and inferiority.[6] Parallel arguments have been made by research that examines the ways in which curriculum promotes particular social-class consciousness, gender consciousness, and other markers of difference in the United States.[7]

Education reflects and shapes our very ways of making sense of who we are and the world in which we live, and therefore can teach people either to self-regulate themselves in a system that privileges only some and/or to challenge that very system. For example, the creation of "Indian boarding schools" in the 19th and 20th centuries for Native Americans explicitly aimed to assimilate students into a racial hierarchy that valued Whites over Natives and that erased Native cultural values and perspectives. The mission of "kill the Indian, save the man" presumed not only that Native cultures were deficient and inferior, but also that Native peoples could only occupy positions of inferiority to Whites. Similarly, public schools in the early to mid-20th century for Asian immigrant students in Hawai`i aimed to Americanize students, by teaching them to "be American" in ways that did not disrupt White privilege in the economy, government, and culture, and in so doing, teaching subservience. Even today, examples abound of curriculum that indirectly teaches students a particular way of fitting into the racial hierarchy of the United States, as with elementary-school Hawaiian history textbooks that contain photographs and stories that look and sound eerily like tourism brochures, as if teaching Native Hawaiian students to see themselves as mere objects of colonial gazes, servants for tourists from the mainland United States, rather than as full participants in American democracy.[8]

Historically, conservatives were among the leading proponents of curriculum standards. American conservatism looks to an idealized past for a sense of who we are and how we should relate to one another, which, in part, involves maintaining or conserving current structures of relationship along the lines of race, social class, gender, and other markers. But recently and particularly within the last decade, neoconservatives have joined the call for curriculum standards. Idealizing not a sense of the past as much as a sense of global superiority, a self-perception as the world's sole remaining superpower, neoconservatism situates conservatism in an era of globalization, an era in which the leading corporations and financial institutions of the American economy strive to dominate economies around the world, with various cultural, educational, communicational, and other institutions colluding to maintain their influence and profit. Under neoconservatism, schools maintain not only racial hierarchies domestically but also cultural and nation-based hierarchies globally. Such was the case soon after September 11, 2001, when various leaders and elected officials criticized educators and entire fields of study—like labor studies, cultural studies, international relations—for teaching students to critique U.S. foreign relations and corporate practices globally and called on schools and universities, instead, to teach in ways that supported the policies of the George W. Bush administration.[9]

Important, here, is how standards-based reform has become operationalized in public schools across the nation. Whereas the ideal of *standards* can embody the highest level of performance, the practice of *standardizing* curriculum and assessments with scripted curriculums and norm-referenced tests reduces learning to a much-narrowed endeavor. This is most visibly the case in schools that do not already have high levels of student achievement. The consequence of not meeting AYP is to make schools look even less like their high-performing counterparts, particularly with less time spent on teaching a range of subject matters like the arts and social studies and more time on only basic reading and mathematics in order to teach to the test and, in more and more instances, to follow scripted curriculum. So, too, with lower-track classrooms, in which students receive even less academic content than their higher-track counterparts. The move toward standards-as-standardization has resulted in curriculum that is more stratified than before and in instruction that is more regulated than before. But such realities get masked by the frame of "standards."

COMPETITION SOLVES ALL

Perhaps the most dominant framing of educational reform today is that competition will solve our problems. Examples include the federal Race to the Top initiative and school-choice programs, which presume that school systems will improve when structured like a marketplace, where schools, teacher preparation programs, educational services, and even teachers compete. The problem is not the system, so the thinking goes, but merely the lack of effort by or knowledge of the individual schools or teachers. Such is the ideology of neoliberalism, which is guiding educational reform not only in the United States but also around the world, including in Australia, Canada, Ethiopia, Japan, Mexico, Namibia, and the United Kingdom.

Whereas classic liberalism places value on the agency of individuals and on freedoms from social and structural restrictions in the pursuit of self-expression and self-actualization, neoliberalism situates such concepts in a market-like economy, asserting that individuals reach their highest potential when put into competition with one another, like businesses in a "free-market" economy, unrestricted by top-down regulations, or at least unrestricted by regulations that aim to level the playing field. Neoliberalism values competitive markets and the freedom of individual choice within them and devalues governmental or cultural attempts to redistribute resources or accountability, often manifesting in policies that reduce governmental regulation of trade, increase the privatization of public services, and support the growth of businesses.

Two aspects of neoliberalism help to advance a pro-business agenda: privatization and personal responsibility. Privatization is the restructuring of public services into a market-like industry that results in the shifting of funds, oversight, and accountability from the government to individuals and corporations. With privatization, economic enterprises become treated as private matters, not under the domain of public, governmental regulation or intrusion, and profit (or loss) becomes a private matter as well, whereby those who choose to work hard and are able to work well should reap the rewards. This latter point is what connects privatization with the commonly expressed values of freedom and meritocracy, thereby making it a policy initiative that reflects American democratic values.

Hand in hand with the concept of privatization is that of personal responsibility, which is the reliance on oneself rather than on others, and consequently the rejection of political or social-welfare structures that could hamper one's own sense of independence and develop, instead, a system of unfair distribution of resources and undeserved rewards. Drawing on classic liberalism's privileging of individual agency and freedom, neoliberalism overlooks structural or institutional biases, historical legacies regarding oppression and injustice, and an economic structure with built-in mechanisms that exacerbate inequalities, such as racial discrimination in employment or tax breaks for the wealthy. Neoliberalism, in other words, promotes an understanding of equality and freedom that presumes a level playing field, and that expects some to win and many others to lose.

Although germinating in the 1940s and 1950s, this ideology and movement began to significantly frame domestic economic policy beginning in the 1980s, as exemplified by the Washington Consensus, which was a set of policy priorities regarding market liberalization, privatization, and fiscal austerity that were created and implemented nationwide and worldwide by the International Monetary Fund, U.S. Treasury, World Bank, and World Trade Organization. The strategy to change public consciousness was threefold: present neoliberal policies as politically neutral concepts of what makes for good management or effective operation—that is, as simply "good" business practice—while obscuring the underlying cultural values and benefits for those in power; change alliances and policy issues while maintaining an underlying neoliberal agenda; and perhaps most important, fuel the debates between Republicans and Democrats on what is "conservative" or "liberal" while masking how both sides of the debate are already framed by neoliberalism.[10]

The success of the neoliberal movement can be understood in large part in terms of its ability to go unquestioned and to be taken for granted as the way things are and should be. Indeed, the Washington Consensus became so taken for granted that, although the U.S. presidency and Congress have since shifted back and forth between being controlled by Republicans and Democrats, U.S. economic policy throughout has remained firmly within neoliberal ideology, supporting policies that, in practice, raise corporate profits and benefit the wealthy at the expense of labor and consumers, thereby exacerbating economic disparities.

This common sense of economic reform had also become the centerpiece of U.S. foreign policy toward economically troubled nations, including Chile and Argentina in the 1970s, Bolivia and China in the 1980s, Russia, South Africa, and South Korea in the 1990s, and Iraq and Sri Lanka in the 2000s, to name just a few. Whether responding to natural disasters or precipitating political coups, the policy was consistent: to withhold U.S. and international financial aid until the nation in need agreed to immediate free-market reform. This Washington Consensus promised a stronger economy, but the immediate removals of governmental regulations alongside the privatizing of public industries that constituted free-market reform consistently led to widespread unemployment and civic strife, followed by repressive governmental action to curtail protest. Such devastation and violation of human and civil rights were possible because, in a crisis, people were and are generally too shocked or fearful to mobilize.

Of course, some people ended up winners. Following each reform, the gap between the haves and the have-nots widened to reflect unprecedented poverty along with record numbers of millionaires and billionaires. In more recent years, this wealth has shifted to multinational corporations led by former U.S. politicians—such as Halliburton, with ties to former Vice President Dick Cheney—hired as contractors to rebuild from the devastation that was sometimes brought about by U.S. foreign policy. That is, corporations are being hired to destroy, and then to rebuild, with failed results in the rebuilding, leading to more turmoil and extremism, thereby justifying more intervention, all without public accountability but at public expense.[11]

The global financial institutions often made educational reform a requirement for broader economic reform, and as a result, neoliberal ideology has similarly framed the reform of public education in countries around the world. Struggling nations could receive financial assistance only if they agreed to deregulate and privatize their public-school systems. As was the case with economic reform, the result was greater disparities. Reforms in Latin American countries in the 1970s, for example, saw what had been almost universal literacy rates drop dramatically.[12]

In the United States, neoliberal ideology did not characterize educational reform until the end of the 20th century. Preceding was the "federal period" of American education, the decades from the 1950s to the 1970s, so-named because of the visible and significant influence of the federal government over public education through the courts and legislation. During this period, the federal government directed its funding to equity programs and formula grants that targeted students who were struggling the most on the basis of family income, gender, English-language proficiency, and disability. But in recent years, and especially with Race to the Top, the federal government has moved toward market solutions and competitive grants.

So, too, has this been apparent at the district level. Reflecting the purported panacea of free-market reform are school-choice movements, including voucher and charter-school initiatives. Chicago's current public-school reform initiative, Renaissance 2010, illustrates this logic that the competition encouraged by school choice will motivate educators to work harder to do better, as will penalties for not meeting standards. Research has shown that Chicago's schools have not improved under Renaissance 2010. Another example of market-based solutions is the proliferation of alternative routes to teacher certification that challenge the "monopoly" of the universities and promise improvement by infusing the market with alternatives. Support for such initiatives continues to grow, despite compelling research revealing their ineffectiveness in improving school performance and teacher quality.[13]

Nonetheless, within this logic, competition is what will make schools and teachers better. Governmental regulation should be kept to a minimum, or at least the appearance of governmental regulation, since not all regulation is unwanted. And therein lies the insidious logic of neoliberalism: Regulation that reflects a social-welfare system, such as tax redistribution, is governmental "intrusion," whereas regulation that benefits those already competing, such as tax breaks for those making the most money, is governmental "support." This double standard often goes unnoticed in neoliberal policies, but it is precisely this contradictory nature of neoliberal policy initiatives that best illustrates how such initiatives can serve to undermine the very things that they purport to strengthen.

In terms of public-school governance, for example, regular neighborhood schools are increasingly required to become more centralized in their governance, more monitored in their performance on standardized tests, more restricted in their spending and hiring, and even more regulated in their curriculum and instruction, as with the increasing use of "teacher-proof," scripted curriculums. In contrast, charter schools are receiving comparatively more autonomy and flexibility in how they operate and account for allocated resources. The freedom of charter schools from many of the regulations placed on regular neighborhood schools raises questions over whether such regulations were intended to improve public schools or were really intended to encourage the creation of alternatives to public education. After all, some charter schools look more like private schools than public schools, with outsourced management, corporate funding, restrictive enrollments, and even religious bases. Seen in this way, the simultaneity of decentralization and privatization, alongside increased regulation of traditional neighborhood schools, suggests that the underlying purpose has been to undermine public education all along.[14]

What is notable, here, is the recognition that the frames of fear, values, standards, and competition overlap in ways that reinforce one another: a state of crisis (fear) makes us seek out reassuring stories of who we are as Americans, increasing the desire to defend commonsensical stories of traditional American values (family values), as we seek out ways to reform schools that build on related values of meritocracy, self-sufficiency, and equity (standards and accountability), and in a context that encourages each of us to do our best (competition).

Clearly, the reality is far more complex than the dominant framings would have us believe. And that is precisely the point—frames have the power to obscure the bigger picture, to narrowly and misleadingly define the problem, and to make imaginable only certain solutions. The commonsensical frames of fear, values, standards, and competition make it easy to overlook the deeper problems and to place all blame on teachers. In turn, the attack on teachers implicate those who are responsible for preparing teachers, which is why many parallel initiatives are underway to undermine teacher preparation.

CHAPTER 3

Less Preparation
Makes for Better Teachers

Soon after college, I returned home to Hawai`i, stocked up on aloha shirts, dug out my box of teaching ideas that I had collected during my years in college and in the Peace Corps, and headed to a high school not far from where I grew up to teach math. I was cocky and eager, but also nervous, because I knew that teaching was exhausting work. Investing the time, energy, and emotions required by that job might quickly get harder to do, I feared, because even my mentors and colleagues were warning me that teaching was a thankless job.

I learned that such was not entirely the case. Yes, some students criticized my classes as boring and my homework as too much and my tests and projects as too hard. Some parents complained that their children were not doing as well as they should, and asked what I was doing about it. Some colleagues and administrators cautioned that too much of my unorthodoxy might generate more criticism and complaints. All this, despite devoting my time during breaks and after-school hours tutoring and advising clubs, working into the nights and weekends on planning, grading, communicating, and looking through my college notes or my colleagues' files for ever more creative and engaging and effective ways to teach.

But some students, even some of the same ones who criticized me, also gave me photos from their proms, or homemade candy for the holidays, or simply a recounting of their latest weekend adventures while hanging out in my classroom during lunch. Parents came to parent-teacher night simply to shake my hand or to see what exactly I was doing that made their child excited about math, or at least excited enough to share their latest three-dimensional project. Colleagues asked to incorporate my ideas into their own teaching. These indirect thank-yous were what kept me going as a teacher.

That was 20 years ago. Today, I have a hard time imagining what could keep me going, because today teaching is not merely a profession that receives little public praise. Rather, it has become a profession that is blamed for all that is wrong with education. Students are not learning? Then it's because teachers are not smart enough, skilled enough, hard-working enough. Gains in student achievement are not sufficient? Create incentives to make teachers work harder, work smarter, and innovate their way to success, all the while regulating and monitoring them. Schools are still failing? Get rid of those teachers.

These are indeed the policy and legislative changes occurring at the local, state, and federal levels. Both Republican and Democratic politicians, including the previous and current U.S. presidents and Secretaries of Education, are blaming the problems in education on teachers, and offering as the panacea the dismissal of teachers as schools get turned around.

Are some teachers lazy and incompetent? Surely, just as in any other profession or industry. Are some teachers part of the reason why some students are struggling in school? It's likely. But placing the blame solely on teachers too narrowly defines the problem and limits the range of possible solutions.

THE SOLUTION IS ON FACEBOOK

In the fall of 2010, Facebook founder Mark Zuckerberg announced a $100 million contribution to improve Newark, NJ, public schools, to support the reforms of Newark mayor Cory Booker toward such market-based reforms as charter schools and teacher merit pay, and was contingent on increasing mayoral control of that school system. Since then, my attention to Facebook has increased. I do not know what compels me to check my Facebook page daily—no, many times a day—since, as my friends will tell you, I almost never post anything or send messages or even read beyond the first few posts on my homepage. Maybe it is my fascination with the ads, and the ones that stand out to me the most are about teaching. Want to become a teacher? From the comfort of your own home? Without quitting your job? Many options exist, as indicated by ads from various online universities that promise initial certification to teach in public schools across the country via programs that are fast-tracked, inexpensive, and online. As I read such ads, I am struck by an underlying message: Becoming a teacher need not involve much in the way of learning to teach. If you know math, you can teach math. To teach, in other words, a person does not need to invest the time to study research, practice with mentors, or hone the knowledge, skills, and dispositions that are specific to teaching.

This characterization that teacher quality is primarily about content knowledge is reflected in current federal legislation that defines the "highly qualified" teacher. The federal government also invests millions of dollars in fast-track alternative teacher preparation programs that offer little or no preservice preparation, including Teach for America, and another program that requires even less preservice preparation, the "Passport to Teaching," offered by the American Board for Certification of Teacher Excellence (ABCTE) (http://www.abcte.org).

The "Passport" awards initial teacher certification based primarily on knowledge of subject matter to be taught. Candidates must hold a bachelor's degree and either have majored in the subject to be taught or have taken a sufficient number of courses in that subject, and they must pass examinations of the subject area and of teaching knowledge that take the form of online, standardized tests. Candidates never need to take courses on, for example, how different students learn, how to design curriculum, how to conduct research on one's own practice, how inequities play out in schools, or how policies and social contexts impact teaching and learning, nor are they required to participate in any supervised, preservice field experience—all of which has been shown by research to increase the ability of teachers to successfully reach struggling students.[1]

Initially in 2002 and 2003, ABCTE had success in getting the credentialing agencies of several states to accept the "Passport" as an alternative route to initial certification for public school teaching. In 2004, ABCTE approached the California Commission on Teacher Credentialing, and that summer, as the commission's hearing on ABCTE approached, a growing number of teacher educators joined with community and advocacy organizations to write letters to newspapers, meet with lawmakers, and attend and testify at the commission's hearing. The commission decided against accepting the "Passport," but the success was bittersweet.

The large number of university faculty members speaking out against ABCTE raised concerns among some community members who responded that the faculty members were being hypocritical. The faculty members were arguing that high-quality teachers are those who have learned not only the subject matter but also how to teach the subject matter, which is not offered in the "Passport" program. But faculties in higher education, including those in teacher preparation programs, teach in a profession that does not require learning how to teach prior to being hired and often bases decisions about hiring and promotions solely or primarily on knowledge and expertise in the subject matter. Higher education was considered by some to be framed by the very definition of teacher quality that the faculties were fighting against, raising questions about why ABCTE was the target of criticism, rather than higher education itself. By challenging the alternative routes, the field of teacher education appeared to be merely protecting the status quo.

"Traditional" routes to initial teacher certification, consisting of university-based coursework and supervised preservice field experiences, have long faced public criticism for being ineffective in preparing teachers. Some of this criticism is internal to the profession: Proponents of "traditional" teacher preparation acknowledge that there is disagreement on the degree to which teacher preparation programs are successful at changing the initial assumptions or preconceptions that prospective teachers have about what teaching is and should be, particularly with regard to diversity and equity. But recent and more dismissive criticism that comes from outside the profession is gaining traction as critics of preservice teacher preparation argue that "traditional" teacher preparation programs create unnecessary barriers that prevent individuals with the knowledge and motivation to teach to become teachers, and therefore, that entirely separate alternative routes should be created.

Research has not shown that alternative, fast-track programs are successful in producing more effective teachers. If anything, research shows the opposite: when teachers are not learning new ideas, they fall back on their own experiences and observations, and turn to common sense, which are often the very ideas and practices that need to be questioned and improved upon.[2] Ending preservice teacher preparation would be removing the very thing that has the potential to change common sense in teaching, and in so doing, to better prepare teachers to teach our increasingly diverse student population. Preservice teacher preparation is not without its problems, but rather than being reduced or eliminated, it should be transformed to center on diversity, equity, and injustice. But this is not the direction in which current reforms are headed.

Current reforms are reducing what teachers need to learn about students, learning, curriculum, assessment, and educational contexts, thereby reducing their ability to understand, create, tailor, and problem-solve. Current reforms are reducing the role of teacher to one of a mere "technician" who can implement the already scripted and authorized curriculum. Grover Whitehurst, while serving as director of the federal Institute for Education Sciences during the George W. Bush administration, argued that we merely need "good enough teachers" who can teach their lessons in order for No Child Left Behind to succeed. Within this logic, "traditional" teacher preparation is both unnecessary and undesired, not only because it is much more costly, but also because it would potentially prepare teachers to challenge the official script. If schools should merely be following the official script, then preparing independent-minded teachers is the problem, not the solution.

The notion that teacher preparation can actually be harmful to education is perhaps most clear in the advocacy of modern-day Christian fundamentalism.

CHURCH AND STATE

From its very beginnings, public education in the United States has been influenced by organized Christianity. When first created, public schools and their predecessors, called "common schools," infused religious instruction throughout the curriculum. This was done directly with moral instruction, typically in the form of Bible readings, and indirectly, as in the most commonly used reading textbooks in the 19th century, the McGuffey Readers, which were filled with stories that taught religious principles (first specifically Calvinist, then general American Protestant). In the mid-19th century, Protestantism was the religious tradition shared among the nation's leading school reformers who sought to significantly shape the structuring of statewide school systems and the content of curriculum, as when prioritizing the development of students' moral character over academic abilities.[3]

Debates over curriculum content have long had religious implication. For example, in the early 20th century, debates over whether to teach evolution or creationism in schools were exemplified in the highly publicized Scopes Trial that took to the Tennessee Supreme Court (which, in turn, successfully affirmed) a state law that forbade teaching evolution, pitting religion against science in determining curriculum content. This debate has continued ever since, as in the 2005 Dover trials, where schools were requiring the teaching of creationism under the frame of "intelligent design," claiming it to be science and, therefore, lawful (the courts did not agree). Battles to include religious instruction extended to higher education as well, as in the 1950s when William Buckley criticized Yale University for spreading "socialist" ideas and created the Intercollegiate Studies Institute, which includes in its mission the interwoven goals of a limited government, free-market economy, and Judeo-Christian values, and which has since spread across the nation to train the next generation of conservative leaders.[4]

The 1960s and 1970s served as a turning point for conservative Christians. The U.S. Supreme Court made several rulings that prohibited certain types of religious instruction in schools; and in particular, declared as unconstitutional state-sponsored prayer in classrooms in 1962, Bible reading as religious instruction in 1963, and state laws that prohibited teaching about evolution in 1968. Starting in the 1970s, with the view that public schools had become increasingly hostile to Christianity, a faction of Christian Fundamentalists turned away from their historical position of political noninvolvement and began to engage in two approaches to change public education: re-Christianization and deinstitutionalization.[5]

Re-Christianization aims to return, maintain, or otherwise increase the presence of state-sponsored religious expression and instruction in public schools. Examples include recent controversies over religious-themed curriculum, particularly those controversies that have reframed controversies from the 1960s, such as when calling creationism "intelligent design," or when calling Bible instruction "equal time" policies, or even when calling comprehensive sexuality education "anti-Christian." Such re-Christianization initiatives have made gains in large part because of the active strategy by the Christian Right throughout the 1980s and 1990s to get their constituents elected onto majorities of school boards across the nation, which in turn endorsed or led such initiatives.

In contrast, deinstitutionalization aims to lessen the educational and political significance of public schools, and to turn to other institutions to educate Christian children. Couched in the ideology of "parental rights," and in line with the goals of the Republican Party, this approach opposes any governmental effort to regulate education, including the very existence of a federal Department of Education, as well as the ratifying of the U.N. Convention on the Rights of the Child, which only the United States and one other nation have yet to do. One such alternative to public schooling is home-schooling, which is also advocated by the Tea Party, and which is supported in large part by for-profit curriculum and service providers, accounting for millions of school-aged children. As with re-Christianization, deinstitutionalization revolves around the notion that public schools should be teaching in ways that reflect Fundamentalist Christian values, or at the least, should not be teaching in contradiction to such. The growth of homeschooling among the Christian Right has coincided with a burgeoning industry to provide Christian-related services and resources for homeschooling parents. In fact, the bulk of available homeschooling materials are Christian-related, and targeted to mothers.[6]

The role of gender, here, is significant. Coinciding with a rejection of the public institution of schools is the reinforcing of the private institution of the home and of traditional gender roles. Although it is true that, through much of history, public school teachers have been predominantly women, the type of women desired as teachers (young or old, married or single, etc.) has varied, depending on the historical context. This has had much to do with the contradictory nature of the teaching profession as one that is viewed as simultaneously strict and nurturing, rational and emotional, secular and spiritual, masculine and feminine, public and private. With the move to homeschooling, women take on a teaching role that reinforces rather than competes with the domestic function of mother, because unlike the schoolteacher, whose identity of public servant often conflicts with that of mother, the homeschooling teacher's identity of religious servant actually intertwines with that of mother. Many of the homeschooling advocates and many of the homeschooling service providers are Christian Right mothers.

The demands of Christian-centered homeschooling have implications for the preparation of teachers, who accordingly should not be receiving preparation for multicultural curriculum, critical pedagogy, and student-centered classrooms. Instead, teachers and curriculum materials should merely be evidencing moral authority, such as when teachers attend the right religious institution and curriculum materials are authored and distributed by the right organizations.

The parent-teachers do not need to undergo instructor training since the curriculum materials are highly scripted, presumably transparent in meaning, credible in content and approach, and most important, buffered from outside influences. The parent-teachers, in other words, embody the deprofessionalization of teaching, the feminization of teaching, and the re-Christianization of teaching, all at once.

Following this logic, preservice teacher preparation is not merely irrelevant, but can actually pose a threat within the framing of the Christian Right; therefore, colleges of education, the homes of the "traditional" teacher preparation programs, have come increasingly under attack.

MONOPOLIES AND MARKETS

The notion that teacher education is itself a market has framed debates on educational reform since the 1980s. In 1988, George H. W. Bush campaigned for the U.S. presidency on a platform that called for alternative routes to teacher certification to remove the "unnecessary barriers" that keep otherwise qualified individuals from teaching. In 1989, the think tank Heritage Foundation argued that the entire enterprise of state teacher certification was "a cartel operated by the teacher unions and colleges of education to enforce monopolies in what amounts to restraint of trade . . . [that] has most surely impaired the quality of teaching in the classroom." In 2005, Chester Finn, former assistant secretary of education under President Reagan, replayed such criticism, arguing that "alternative routes to the teaching profession have arisen to challenge the monopolistic hold of the ed[ucational] school cartel." Such criticisms reflect just how significantly the debate on educational reform, and teacher education in particular, has come to be framed by the metaphor of markets.[7]

Simultaneous to the framing of markets is the conceptual shift away from institutional change to individual change. During the 1990s and 2000s, organizations such as the Fordham Foundation increasingly moved the debates on teacher education from institutional authority for certification to individual merit based on test outcomes. This shift has political significance because attention to individual performance detracts from deeper, structural reasons for educational inequity. Simply put, the new common sense tells us that improving education means raising test scores, and that raising test scores is possible when teachers know the content. Individual performance, within this logic, is attributed to knowing what to teach versus ever learning how to teach, which makes "traditional" teacher preparation not only irrelevant, but an unnecessary hurdle that keeps away the best and brightest.

Consequently, the federal government has turned its attention to removing "barriers" to teacher recruitment and opening the door to alternative routes to certification, particularly as the definition of teacher quality and teacher qualification became less linked to preparation, and more linked to subject matter competency, as happened in the 1998 reauthorization of the Higher Education Act, and is being debated in 2011 in the reauthorization of NCLB. In fact, when NCLB was first launched in 2001, President George W. Bush framed educational reform not in terms of structural reform, but rather, in terms of needing more high-quality teachers, which he defined as teachers who merely know the subject matter.

Under the guise of a market that would encourage competition and drive improvement, a two-track system has emerged that supports fast-track programs while overburdening traditional programs. Specifically, the push to produce teachers who are, according to NCLB, "highly qualified," has resulted in more and more requirements and restrictions for "traditional" teacher preparation programs at the same time that alternative-certification programs like ABCTE and Teach for America are receiving more and more autonomy and flexibility, as well as federal funding. That is, at the same time that policy makers ask teacher preparation programs in higher education to do more to prepare teachers for certification, including more documentation to reflect meeting more standards, they authorize and fund fast-track programs that, by definition and design, do less. This contradiction functions not to raise the quality of teachers, but to undermine teacher preparation in higher education altogether, since preservice teachers receive less, not more preparation from both the fast-track programs and the "traditional" programs that must now divert enormous resources to documenting that they meet the increasing requirements and restrictions.

The graduates of such programs also follow two tracks. Teachers receiving traditional preparation are more likely to be teaching in prosperous suburban and elite-urban public schools, whereas teachers from fast-track alternative preparation programs are far more likely to teach in struggling schools serving students who are predominantly working-class and/ or people of color. This situation is not unique to the United States. The World Bank and International Monetary Fund have led educational reforms in nations around the world, including in Latin America and West Africa, with exactly the same result: struggling schools are hiring teachers with less preparation, lower pay and benefits, and harsher working conditions. Less credentialed and more transitory, such teachers also have less capacity to organize for better salaries and working conditions for themselves and their students.[8]

And perhaps that is the point. Perhaps the creation of fast-track alternative teacher preparation programs was never meant to improve teacher quality overall. After all, the most elite schools are not recruiting from the fast-track programs. Fast-track alternative teacher preparation programs exist primarily for schools with large percentages of students of color and students living in poverty, suggesting that such reforms target only certain groups of students, with only certain outcomes expected.

In particular, this two-track system plays a pivotal role in maintaining an economy that is characterized by vast disparities in wealth. Despite the popular reference to the "information age" or "technological societies," the majority of jobs emerging around the world, including in the United States, do not and will not require a level of education beyond elementary schooling, and therefore, most teachers need not be well-trained. To do otherwise, according to this logic, is a waste of resources.[9]

The attack on university-based teacher education found much amplification in a speech given by Secretary of Education Duncan on October 2009, in which he claimed that, "by almost any standard, many if not most of the nation's 1,450 schools, colleges, and departments of education are doing a mediocre job of preparing teachers for the realities of the 21st century classroom."[10] He did not explain what research would allow such a blanket statement, or what standards he used, or what he meant by "mediocre" or "realities." But therein began a rapidly evolving national dialogue about whether university-based teacher preparation programs are mediocre, whether the teachers they produce are mediocre, and what it would mean to evaluate such claims.

So, too, began concerted efforts to further regulate university-based teacher preparation programs under the guise of evaluating their efficacy. At least three conceptualizations of preparation quality are driving such efforts at program evaluation.

First, quality is determined by what programs do. Such is the focus of an evaluation of 1,000 teacher preparation programs currently under way jointly by the National Council on Teacher Quality (NCTQ) and *U.S. News & World Report*, which focuses on course syllabi and several other indicators of what programs say that they do. Criticisms about this narrow definition of efficacy, along with additional concerns about research methodology, have led several coalitions of university administrators to write joint letters to NCTQ and *U.S. News* to urge a more comprehensive, valid, fair, and theoretically grounded method of evaluation. This evaluation has not proceeded collaboratively with the teacher preparation programs, which raises questions about whether the underlying intent is to formatively assess with the goal of improving, or to summarily dismiss by providing data to support a foregone conclusion.

Second, quality is determined by what students do. A decade ago, some of the California university-based teacher preparation programs began to develop and pilot a performance-based assessment of preservice teachers, the Performance Assessment for California Teachers, or PACT (www.pacttpa.org). The PACT was developed in response to calls for a certification process that does not rely predominantly on meeting course and fieldwork requirements, and as an alternative to the state-produced performance assessment tool (i.e., the Teacher Performance Assessment, or TPA). The PACT consists of a portfolio of materials demonstrating teaching preparedness, including sample lessons with rationale and illustrative materials like a video documentation and student work.

Criticisms emerged early on about ways in which the PACT required that programs teach to the PACT, with teacher educators focusing enormous amounts of time preparing student teachers for documentation rather than on learning to teach, and with student teachers intentionally performing and producing what they believe the external reviewers will review positively, echoing criticisms of high-stakes testing for students that results in merely teaching to and performing for the tests. Additional criticisms arose about the scoring of the portfolios by external reviewers who are seeing merely a snapshot of teaching that cannot possibly encompass the many indicators of quality teaching that would or should be known in a fair and accurate assessment of teacher preparedness. Whether intentional or not, the impact of the PACT is to deprofessionalize both teaching and teacher preparation. Research has not shown the PACT to be an effective or accurate tool for increasing teacher quality, yet the PACT is now spreading nationwide.[11]

Third, quality is determined by how future teachers perform. Proposed federal legislation is focusing on the opposite end of the teacher preparation process by tying student test scores to the quality of their teachers, which in turn are tied back to the quality of the teachers' preparation programs. That is, effective teacher preparation programs are those that produce teachers who can raise student test scores, and both increased funding and reduced regulation would incentivize programs to demonstrate such output. Such legislation builds solidly on the ideology of testing described earlier, which purports that learning means high test scores, teaching means raising those scores, and learning to teach means learning to raise those scores.

Research has shown that incentivizing teacher salaries by tying teacher evaluation to student test scores does not raise the quality of instruction or student achievement.[12] So, too, with other reforms, like turnaround school policies, high-stakes testing for promotion and graduation, school-choice and voucher programs—none are supported by research. At a time when the rhetoric of educational reform calls for evidence-based, data-driven decision making, the lack of research to support the reforms described here certainly raises the question of "Why?" Why are Americans so compelled to buy into these proposals?

If facts are not driving decision making, then something else, something more compelling is. Understanding educational reform requires understanding who is pushing for these reforms and with what incentives. We need to follow the money.

CHAPTER 4

When Billionaires Become Educational Experts

A few years ago, when still in my 30s, I was on several different prescription medications: for high cholesterol, skin problems, sleep problems, and others. My healthcare seemed increasingly guided by philosophies of treating the symptoms (with pills) and generating more profits (for drug companies, for my healthcare providers). I remember the day when I brought home yet another prescription, and after staring in disbelief at my growing pile of pill bottles, decided that I needed to take a different route. I began a journey toward improving my health and well-being more naturally. Learning from various alternative and integrative medicines, I adopted radical changes in what I eat, how I exercise, and why I engage in other forms of self-care, with improvements that even my doctors found surprising. I continue that journey today.

I was quite fortunate: I had supportive healthcare professionals to turn to, I had the financial resources to access many of the services that I wanted, I had the time and skills to research different options and risks, and I had the social network to support me. At a time when debates were raging nationwide about how to increase access to health insurance in order to improve healthcare provision, I often wondered what would have happened had my fortunes been different. In particular, what if decisions about my healthcare and the options available to me were made by individuals whose primary concern was their own profits, rather than by my doctors who know my needs and who support the kinds of "alternative" programs that I wanted to pursue, which, for the most part, are far less profitable than my previous regiment of pills and sessions?

For years, critics have pointed to the decreasing ability of healthcare professionals to make decisions and provide services because of the demands of insurance companies and health management organizations to sustain profits. Healthcare decisions are increasingly being made by the wrong people and for the wrong reasons.

So, too, with public education. Current reforms are allowing certain individuals with neither scholarly nor practical expertise in education to exert significant influence over educational policy for communities and children other than their own. They, the millionaires and billionaires from the philanthropic and corporate sectors, are experimenting in urban school districts with initiatives that lack sound evidence about their viability and usefulness, often with failed results in those schools, and yet their influence is growing. Funding for public education is shrinking, and additional monies must come from somewhere, and consequently, for those with wealth, there is much influence to be had over public education.

There is also much profit to be earned from public education. The American educational system today is a $500 to $600 billion enterprise, funded overwhelmingly by public dollars, with billions of dollars in services and products being outsourced, and with political lobbying groups like the Democrats for Education Reform (DFER), financed by hedge-fund millionaires who are leading the push to further outsource. The public educational system has always had ties to the business sector, and has always received both funding and regulation from the business sector, including business leaders themselves and the philanthropies funded by business fortunes. But that influence has not always looked the same. In particular, in recent years a handful of million-aires and billionaires have come to exert influence over edu-cational policy and practice like no other time in American history, despite the fact that philanthropic giving has always constituted less than 1% of total educational funding. What has happened? The role of business and philanthropy has shifted, reconfigured, and converged over the past century, and therefore, seeing the bigger picture of public education requires understanding the interrelated histories of philan-thropic and corporate influence.

TRADITIONAL PHILANTHROPY AND EARLY CORPORATE INFLUENCE

Philanthropies have a long history of giving to public educa-tion, including the philanthropies of White businessmen that shaped the education of early communities of color. Follow-ing the U.S. Civil War, for example, philanthropies helped to establish primary and vocational schools for African Ameri-cans in the South, as well as normal schools that eventual-ly became Black colleges and universities, which expanded access even as they reinforced segregated and differentiated learning. In the first half of the 20th century, philanthropies supported and expanded the use of intelligence testing that justified a racialized understanding of what different groups of students could learn and do, making commonsensical the notion of academic tracking. Clearly, the early philanthropies were varied in their goals and impact, funding initiatives that both reinforced and challenged inequities in education. But perhaps the most well-known of the early philanthropies, which were the Carnegie Corporation, Ford Foundation, and Rockefeller Foundation, increasingly tried to raise visibility of

educational inequities, thus making the mainstream perception of traditional philanthropy increasingly liberal and altruistic for much of the 20th century.[1]

The business sector also has a long history of influencing
public education, particularly from the period of 1890–1940,
when public schools were consolidating into larger and
larger school districts. As cities became increasingly diverse
from immigration, and as members of the working class
won more and more seats on city governments, the business
elite made concerted efforts to take control of local school
boards, not only by getting business leaders elected onto
school boards, but also by structuring the boards to reflect
the centralized control and bureaucracy that characterized
the large industries that were emerging at this time. That is,
the business elite influenced school governance not only by
constituting its governing bodies but also by structuring its
model of management. The business elite turned their attention to higher education as well, as in the 1950s when the
U.S. Chamber of Commerce and corporate advocates began
creating a network of organizations on university campuses
which aimed to cultivate probusiness values in the next generation of leaders.[2]

PHILANTHROPY AND BUSINESS ROUNDTABLES

As the United States entered the second half of the 20th century, significant economic, legal, cultural, and ideological
changes occurred that would prompt the formation of new
structures in both the philanthropic and the corporate sectors.
In the early 1970s, two national groups emerged that would
have enormous influence in the decades to follow on public
policy generally, and educational policy in particular: the Philanthropy Roundtable and the Business Roundtable.

First, let me discuss the Philanthropy Roundtable. The 1950s and 1960s was a time of numerous and significant legal and cultural changes in the United States regarding inequities of race, social class, gender, and other social markers. The Civil Rights Movement brought together a range of constituents to push for landmark legislation and policy changes across the nation. To opponents of the Civil Rights Movement, such attempts at resource redistribution and governmental regulation departed from the American ideals of self-sufficiency and meritocracy, and in the process, threatened to weaken the American economic system of "free enterprise." Opponents also took note of how such legal changes were led by a "liberal establishment" that was organized and strategic in ways that conservatives were not yet.

In 1971, Lewis Powell, who would soon after become an associate justice on the U.S. Supreme Court, wrote a memo that was internal to the U.S. Chamber of Commerce, known as the "Powell Manifesto." This memo described a concerted liberal attack on the American "free enterprise" system and on American democracy itself, and successfully called for organizing and action. In response to the Powell manifesto, a group of conservatives, particularly philanthropists with family business fortunes, came together and formed a national Philanthropy Roundtable, which would strategize about how to use their funding for conservative movement building.

At the helm were wealthy conservatives whose philanthropic work helped to seed what eventually grew into an interconnected web of organizations and initiatives. Their project was as much legislative as it was ideological, in that they aimed to impact legislation and policy as well as to shape common sense in society. In the decades to follow, the conservative philanthropies developed interconnected funding priorities and strategies to advance public-policy agendas that were probusiness and anti-social welfare, and that would enable the American political and economic systems to continue to benefit those racial and social-class groups that were already privileged in society.

The priorities were to develop four things: a cadre of students in higher education who embrace conservative ideologies, a generation of scholars who produce research that makes conservative ideologies accessible and who then enter government service, a network of regional and state policy think tanks and advocacy organizations, and a protocol for using media to reach the public effectively.[3] Their strategies have been quite successful, as evidenced by the emergence of such educational and government leaders as Dinesh D'Souza, Chester Finn, Newt Gingrich, Thomas Sowell, and until recently, Diane Ravitch, who were once beneficiaries of fellowships and other forms of professional support from the philanthropies, as well as the preponderance of messages in the media and legislation that were developed in related think tanks.

At the top of the chopping block was public education, considered by some to be a drain on the government and a crutch for society, not only because it was the most expensive of domestic enterprises but also because it exemplified a socialist enterprise. Conservatives called for the entire school system to be privatized, made into a free enterprise, and the conservatives' strategy of choice was school vouchers. Early on, Milton Friedman, one of the leading proponents of free market reform, argued that, "Vouchers are not an end in themselves; they are a means to make a transition from a government to a free-market system." Not surprisingly, the focus of many conservative foundations has been and continues to be school choice and school-voucher initiatives.

Until recently the four most influential conservative foundations nationally were the Bradley, Olin, Scaife, and Smith Richardson foundations, sometimes dubbed the "Four Sisters." The Lynde and Harry Bradley Foundation in

Wisconsin is the country's largest conservative foundation, and includes among its priorities the ending of affirmative action and of welfare. A former board member is William Bennett, Secretary of Education under President Reagan, and the Bradley Foundation is involved in various educational policy initiatives, including the support of school-voucher programs and privatization. The John M. Olin Foundation, ceased in 2005, focused on developing research through think tanks as well as through higher education, with large gifts to Harvard, Yale, the University of Chicago, and other universities, as well as to individual researchers. The Scaife Family Foundations, consisting of the Sarah Scaife, Allegheny, and Carthage Foundations, funded by the Mellon family fortune, gives to a range of think tanks and lobbying and publishing groups. According to its website, the H. Smith Richardson Foundation in North Carolina supports the "next generation of public policy researchers and analysts" by funding think tanks and universities. All four Sisters have contributed funding to the leading conservative think tanks, including the American Enterprise Institute for Public Policy, the Heritage Foundation, and the Hoover Institution.

Several other foundations gave over $100 million to conservative causes between 1998 and 2004, including the Walton Family and DeVos foundations. Created by the heirs of Sam Walton of Walmart, the world's largest corporation, the Walton Family Foundation in Arkansas has financed nearly every ballot initiative for vouchers since 1993. Walton funds such pro-voucher organizations as the Alliance for School Choice, as well as organizations that draw communities of color into the pro-voucher movement, such as the Black Alliance for Educational Options and the Hispanic Council for Reform and Educational Options. The Richard and Helen DeVos Foundation in Michigan, funded by the AmWay fortune, supports vouchers as well as organizations of the Christian

Right, including Focus on the Family, that have vast media and communications resources. More recently, the Charles Koch Foundation has targeted higher education by funding faculty positions, think tanks, and educational initiatives in universities across the country. The websites of Media Matters Action Network (http://mediamattersaction.org) and People for the American Way (http://www.pfaw.org) provide descriptions of these and numerous other such foundations.

Of course, conservative foundations are not the only ones funding education. Liberal philanthropies that identify with the goals and legacy of the Civil Rights Movement also contribute to education, but they are far less visible and influential in changing federal or state-level policy. Perhaps the most notable strategic difference between conservative and liberal philanthropic organizations is the expectation placed on how organizations will use their funds. Whereas the liberal philanthropies tend to fund a large number of organizations for specific projects of limited term and scope, the conservative ones are more likely to fund the general operations of a smaller number of organizations over longer periods of time in order to build institutional infrastructure. The conservative foundations especially target funding to organizations that aggressively lobby in state legislatures and Congress, and that engage effectively in media campaigns, thus ensuring that their ideas are enacted into law with public support. Consequently, the conservative movement has emerged as an interconnected web of organizations with aligned missions and coordinated strategies, often facilitated by shared board members.[4]

The history and function of the Philanthropy Roundtable parallels those of the Business Roundtable. The 1960s was a time of declining corporate profits, resulting from such factors as deficit spending to fund the war in Vietnam, rising oil prices following the formation of OPEC, and an increasingly competitive market in a globalizing economy.[5] It was also a time of increasing governmental regulation of the workplace and increasing influence of organized labor. In response, some business leaders felt the need to organize the corporate sector in order to influence public policy in ways that advanced corporate interests, particularly the interests of the business elite. In 1972 the Business Roundtable formed, consisting of the top 300 CEOs in the nation.

The Business Roundtable had always addressed a range of public policies, but in the late 1980s it began focusing significant attention on public education. In 1989, it called for six "national education goals" and, soon after, nine "essential components of a successful education system." This call put pressure on states to move toward an outcomes-based model of educational reform, using standardized tests to measure student and teacher performance, with sanctions and rewards for failure or success. Reinforcing the pressure put on states was a large network of influential foundations, centers, universities, and public media assembled by the Roundtable, that consisted of such entities as the Annenberg Center, Broad Foundation, Education Trust, Harvard Graduate School, and most newspaper editorial boards.

In so doing, the Business Roundtable effectively laid out a blueprint for standards-based reform, begun during the Reagan administration but culminating in No Child Left Behind (NCLB), that has become so taken-for-granted as the way to think about education quality and educational reform that even Democrats, from Clinton onward, have put forth proposals that were framed by these concepts.

VENTURE PHILANTHROPY

As the United States neared the end of the 20th century, the globalizing economy provided fertile ground for an unprecedented accumulation of wealth by the corporate elite, reflecting the largest wealth gap between the rich and the poor in American history. Taking this new wealth and the lessons learned about leveraging wealth for both increased profits and political influence, several of these millionaires and billionaires transformed the landscape of philanthropy, developing a new type that operates much more like the conservative foundations than traditional philanthropies. These are the venture philanthropies.[6]

Unlike traditional philanthropy, which sought to—at least in principal—"give back" to society, venture philanthropy parallels venture capitalism with the goal of investing capital in ways that earn more. In contrast to venture capitalism, one benefit of venture philanthropy is that it operates under different incorporation laws, providing tax shelter for what are really financial investments. Whereas the financial returns may not be as immediate as in corporate transactions, the policy foci of today's venture philanthropists indeed reveals the economic incentive of their investments. They are pushing overwhelmingly for the privatization of public education, creating new markets of hundreds of billions of dollars, as well as for the prerogative to direct how public tax dollars gets spent. They target the large urban school districts, experimenting with models that eventually will scale up nationally, as is the case in Chicago, where the Gates Foundation alone has spent millions on small-school initiatives, school turnarounds, youth organizing, and parent organizing.[7]

Another departure from traditional philanthropy is the role that venture philanthropists play in their investments. Whereas traditional philanthropists view their giving as donations that support what others were doing, venture philanthropists view their giving as entryways into that work. That is, philanthropists themselves are now getting significantly involved in goal setting, decision making, and evaluating progress and outcomes to ensure that their priorities are met. This hands-on role of the venture philanthropists allows them to more directly and substantially impact public policy, particularly in a climate where their financial aid is so desperately needed.

Indeed, the timing was fortuitous for venture philanthropy. Setting the stage was the 1983 report by the Reagan administration, *A Nation at Risk,* which claimed not only that public schools were failing, but more significantly, that their failure was a primary cause of the nation's economic recession at that time. Such a crisis gave the business elite yet another reason to turn their attention to public education. And for their part, educational leaders needed the additional funding because less and less tax dollars were being earmarked for education, which was a trend that has spanned decades. States have been disinvesting in education: Over the past 20 years in Illinois, for example, state contributions to public higher education dropped from almost 50% to less than 20% of university budgets. Cities and districts have also been disinvesting: Beginning in the 1980s and lasting through the 1990s the federal government reduced its funding to cities, and when combined with the global financial crisis of the past few years, cities and districts found new justification to further slash education budgets, resulting in the current furloughs of public school teachers and staff, shortened school years, reduced services and resources, and an impaired quality of education. This was not only the result of less money, caused in large part by dramatically decreasing taxes paid by corporations and the wealthy, but also the result of less priority being placed on education, at a time when budgets for prisons and wars have been steadily increasing.

Such cuts, of course, disproportionately impact students of color and working-class students, who are the ones who disproportionately populate the public schools and public universities, which brings us full circle to the time of the early philanthropies when wealthy White businessmen were using their wealth to change the education of primarily poorer students of color, often with even greater disparities resulting. The change is not only in educational policy, but also in public-policy decision making more broadly, signaling the transition from public deliberation by an elected government to decisions of self-appointed individuals with no accountability to the public.

The two leading venture philanthropies, the Gates Foundation and the Broad Foundation, do include among their grantees historically liberal organizations like teacher unions. However, their funding priorities and strategic initiatives are so framed by neoliberalism, and their partnerships with conservative organizations and leaders so extensive, that their impact is indistinguishable from the conservative foundations. Overwhelmingly, by number of initiatives and amount of funding, the leading venture philanthropies are prioritizing the privatization and marketization of public education, with such initiatives as outsourcing of school management, which can best be seen in school districts that are targeted for charter-school growth, where the majority of charter schools are managed by for-profit companies; incentive pay for teachers; alternative routes to certification for teachers and school leaders; and school choice and charter school initiatives. The leading venture philanthropies are investing in a web of organizations not unlike the web of foundations, think tanks, media organizations, and advocacy groups that characterizes the conservative network. For example, The Gates Foundation funds think tanks like the American Enterprise Institute to issue reports; communications groups like Teach Plus to amplify the voices of teachers who specifically counter the voices of the teacher unions; and leadership groups like the National Governors Association and the Council of Chief State School Officers to develop policies around the common core standards.

The top-giving venture philanthropies include a broad mix of foundations from family fortunes: the Broad Education Foundation, the Bill and Melinda Gates Foundation, the Walton Family Foundation, the Michael and Susan Dell Foundation, the Donald and Doris Fisher Fund, and the Lynde and Harry Bradley Foundation. These mega-philanthropies are funding other education-related venture philanthropies, like the Charter School Growth Fund and the NewSchools Venture Fund. Venture philanthropies include not only the national foundations from individual family fortunes, but also the local philanthropies that were founded by collectives of business leaders, as is the case in Chicago with the Chicago Public Education Fund and the Renaissance Schools Fund. Chicago has much to show with regard to the role of philanthropies and corporations in transforming education because it has become a testing ground for how to leverage wealth to transform public education.

SEEING THE CONNECTIONS: LEVERAGING WEALTH IN CHICAGO

During the Reagan administration, then Secretary of Education William Bennett came to Chicago to call its schools the worst in the nation. A decade later the tide changed, and in 1995 President Clinton called Chicago "a model for the nation" on school reform, a sentiment that echoes more loudly today as the current Secretary of Education and former CEO of Chicago Public Schools Arne Duncan brings to scale nationwide the reforms that he tested in Chicago, what some people call the "Chicago miracle."

The catalyst for the "Chicago miracle" is Renaissance 2010, an initiative launched in 2004 that aimed to open 100 new smaller schools and close about 60 "failing" schools by the year 2010. At the center of Renaissance 2010 is the "turn-around" strategy, which reforms schools by replacing the leaders and teachers, or simply closing the schools and opening others in their place. To date, 75 new schools have opened, and research shows the results of Renaissance 2010 to be flat or negative. Many of the new schools are charter schools that serve fewer low-income, limited English language proficient, and disabled students than regular neighborhood public schools. More than a third of them are in communities that are not high-needs areas. Districtwide high-school test scores have not risen, and most of the lowest performing high schools saw scores drop.[8]

What is important, here, is the recognition that Renaissance 2010 did not emerge from conversations about how to better address inequities and disparities in education, but rather in conversations about increasing corporate profits in Chicago. The blueprint of Renaissance 2010 lies in a report entitled *Left Behind*, released a year earlier by the Commercial Club of Chicago, which mapped out a strategy for schools to align more closely with the goals of the business elite. Central to that blueprint was the creation of 100 new charter schools, managed by for-profit businesses, and freed from legal mandates to have Local School Councils, teacher unions, and even, in some of these schools, certified teachers.

Renaissance 2010 coincided with the proliferation of pathways to certifying and hiring new teachers with little or no preservice preparation, reflecting the global trend of linking the restructuring of education around corporate needs with the devaluing of professional preparation of teachers, and funded by some of the very people who had been pushing for Renaissance 2010. The turnaround strategy blamed student failure on incompetent teachers, with the implication that current teachers be fired as new pathways to teaching are created. By far, the pathways of choice were the fast-track alternative teacher preparation programs, which proliferated and enjoyed rapidly increased funding from both opponents of public education and proponents alike.

Fast-track alternative teacher-certification programs are not new to Chicago. The Golden Apple Scholar Program (http://www.goldenapple.org) was started in 1989 and currently prepares teachers for initial certification with a summer of coursework followed by a teacher residency. Teach for America started outside of Chicago in 1990 as a small program that offered a summer of coursework and additional coursework during the subsequent 2-year teaching commitment in high-needs schools and quickly expanded to cities across the nation, currently housing one of its main regional offices in Chicago, and including among its major funders the Broad Foundation, the Michael and Susan Dell Foundation, the Doris and Donald Fisher Fund, the Rainwater Charitable Funds, and the federal government via AmeriCorps and the U.S. Department of Education (http://www.teachforamerica.org).

Over the past few years, Chicago Public Schools has opened the doors to a wider range of alternative, fast-track routes, including online programs, summer programs that lead to temporary licensure, and residency programs. For example, one program that mirrors Teach for America is the Chicago Teaching Fellows Program (http://chicagoteachingfellows.org), created in 2006 with federal funding, which places teachers in classrooms following a summer of initial coursework and alongside continuing coursework. The Chicago Teaching Fellows Program was created by the New Teachers Project, formerly run by Michelle Rhee, who was recently chancellor of DC Public Schools, and including on its board of directors Wendy Kopp of Teach for America. Concordia University–Chicago (http://www.cuchicago.edu), which has offered certification programs for decades, is seeing rapidly increasing enrollments with its online programs that cost less to run, in part by outsourcing its instruction to doctoral students from surrounding universities. A similar program is the American College of Education (http://www.ace.edu), created in 2004, which includes on its board of directors former U.S. Secretary of Education Rod Paige, and which offers an inexpensive 1-year, fully online certification program.

The Academy for Urban School Leadership (AUSL), formed in 2001 by venture capitalist Martin Koldyke (who also founded the Golden Apple Foundation, which runs the Golden Apple Scholar Program), partners with local universities to offer the Urban Teacher Residency program, which consists of a teacher residency alongside coursework, and includes among its major funders the Bill and Melinda Gates Foundation, the Michael and Susan Dell Foundation, the MetLife and Motorola Foundations, and the NewSchools Venture Fund. Koldyke and another AUSL board member, Cordelia Meyer, are leaders in the Commercial Club of Chicago.

Funded by millions of dollars from various foundations and the federal government, some of these programs also enjoy privileges from Chicago Public Schools, including reserved slots in the hiring process for their participants or graduates, as was recently the case for Teach for America.

A 2011 study by *Newsweek* and the Center for Public Integrity revealed that, despite the billions of dollars invested by the top four philanthropies over the past decade, the ten

top-receiving urban districts showed little gains. Yet these investors continue to be driving education reform.[9]

An illuminating example of money driving reform occurred in June 2011 in Illinois, where legislation passed with
overwhelming support from both Republicans and Democrats
that capitalized on the notion that teachers and unions are to
blame for school failure in order to justify, among other things,
weakening collective bargaining rights. This legislation was
pushed by the advocacy group Stand for Children with millions of dollars in private donations by the city's elite. Among
the dozens of Chicago philanthropists who funded and/or
supported Stand for Children were Penny Pritzker, whose
family founded the Hyatt hotel chain, who was a chief fund-
raiser for the 2008 Obama campaign, who served as former
chair of the Chicago Public Education Fund, and is currently a
member of the Chicago school board; and Bruce Rauner, chair
of the board of the Chicago Public Education Fund and head
of strategic planning for the Renaissance Schools Fund, and
education chair of the Civic Committee of the Commercial
Club of Chicago.

In listing these various contributing individuals and foundations, it is important to note that, although the vision for
current reforms have roots in conservative foundations and
corporate networks, the current players who are leveraging
wealth to push these reforms into policy and legislation include both Republicans and Democrats. In fact, the majority
of the individuals making large contributions to Stand for
Children in the months preceding the 2011 Illinois legislation
were Democrats, making all the more clear how commonsensical certain stories have become about the problems and solutions for public schools.

America's children are in dire need of leaders who can see
the bigger picture and see beyond the dominant frames to

find viable alternatives. America's children deserve schools and initiatives that are shaped by people who bring scholarly and practical expertise in education and a commitment to addressing inequities and injustices, not people who are merely leveraging their wealth to experiment with reforms of other people's schools, or who are merely following the common sense of educational reform. Each and every American has a role to play in advocating for a truly democratic society and a truly educative school system. The time has come to build a movement to reclaim public education.

Reclaiming Public Education

After a particularly rambling conversation in which I tried to explain the goals of this book, a friend pushed me to condense: "If you had only five minutes on *Oprah*, what would you say?" The long-running Oprah Winfrey show has now ended, but the question prompted me to sum up my findings and arguments in three overarching questions that I find useful for assessing current reforms, holding our elected leaders accountable, and imagining better alternatives.

FIVE MINUTES ON *OPRAH*

First, *Are current reforms making America's schools look more like the best schools in our nation and the world, or are they further widening the gap?* Here in Chicago, for example, we can think about the types of public schools that are held up as models for reform, such as the "selective enrollment" schools, or the expensive and elite private schools where politicians and wealthy families send their children, such as the school where President Obama and Mayor Rahm Emanuel sent their children (University of Chicago Lab Schools). These schools are well resourced with up-to-date curriculum materials, advanced laboratories, safe and healthful facilities, opportunities for extracurricular activities, and small class sizes; staffed with well educated, experienced, supported, and well compensated teachers and administrators. They are also centered on rich, broad, interdisciplinary curriculums that are developed by the teachers and grounded in research, as well as complex assessments that support teachers in tailoring their instruction to their students' needs. These are not the characteristics that current reforms are prioritizing or even acknowledging. The blaming of teachers goes hand-in-hand with the current national obsession with high-stakes testing, turnaround-school policy, marketization and privatization of schooling, narrowing of curriculum, lessening of teacher preparation, and experimentation of school reforms by investors, which all are making schools look less and less like the best schools and less and less like what America's children need and deserve. Reforms are leading schools in the wrong direction. This is not to say that the most prestigious schools are not also in need of improvement—indeed, I would argue that all schools can be better—but if we truly want the best for every child, then shouldn't these schools be the minimum standards for America's schools, rather than the exceptions?

Second, *Are current reforms building on sound research, or do they fall back on common sense?* Common sense is not always supported by research. Common sense tells us, for example, that if students are struggling with reading and mathematics, then schools need to cut out the other subjects and focus on the basic skills, laying a solid foundation before advancing to other subjects. But research tells us otherwise: Students actually learn basic reading better when reading in context and across the disciplines than when only drilling on basic skills, and similarly, learn basic mathematics better when applying mathematics to solve complex problems than when only drilling on basic skills. From high-stakes testing of students to performance pay for teachers, from turnaround policies for schools to choice programs for parents, from less preparation for teachers to for-profit management of schools, current reforms not only lack a research basis, but more important, have already been proven to lead to widened disparities. Of course, research is a vastly diverse enterprise: researchers are asking different questions, using different methods, and drawing various conclusions that can be used to justify any range of policies. But such variance only reinforces the importance of looking broadly at the field of research, being skeptical of its claims, demanding that its analysis be thorough and rigorous, and questioning the ethics of any of its implications. That is, we need to delve even more deeply into research, not less.

Third, *Are current reforms guided by a vision in which all of America's children can flourish, or are they framed by a commonsensical story that has led to the opposite outcome?* Perhaps the most salient story today is that of competition solving all problems. Our nation's obsession with competition—students being ranked against one another, states racing to the top, nations outperforming one another—presumes that one can succeed only if others fail. But competition does not always raise the bar. The level of inquiry in a classroom can go up when all students are supported and engaged, which means that the success of one child is greater when others around that child are also succeeding. Similarly, the production of and access to resources can increase when cities and states support and collaborate with one another, rather than separate and compete. The African proverb that "it takes a village to raise a child" offers an alternative vision to guide educational reform that counters the common sense of competition. Here is where, as a nation, we need to think deeply about what we really want for our children, what we really believe are our core values as a democracy.

Seeing the bigger picture, drawing on solid research, articulating a better vision—these are important blocks upon which to build a movement to reclaim public education. And these were exactly the blocks that a group of us in Chicago have been using in our own effort to intervene as scholars and to bring research to bear on Chicago school reform. The following is an account of that effort that I co-wrote in the summer of 2011 with several colleagues: William Ayers, Erica Meiners, Therese Quinn, and David Stovall.

CHICAGO AT A "TEACHABLE MOMENT"

When Richard J. Daley, the longest sitting mayor in Chicago history and the first to voluntarily vacate the office in half a century, announced that he would not seek reelection as mayor of Chicago, residents of every background and political orientation experienced a kind of collective lightheadedness. The political moment—part hope, part fear, and part giddy speculation—opened a floodgate: Veteran politicians as well as novices rushed to create exploratory committees and began gathering petitions and raising money for possible campaigns; community organizers mapped strategies to mobilize people around key issues; artists and activists came together in imaginative interventions. The possibility for dramatic changes in Chicago A.D. (After Daley) was a dizzying and seductive prospect.

And yet candidates across the board, when asked about their policies concerning education and public schools, betrayed a lack of vision and imagination, and most disturbing of all, displayed little knowledge about the basic realities of Chicago schools or of the initiatives that might actually improve them. They responded instead with clichés, conventional thinking, and "received wisdom": We should fire the bad teachers and focus all available energy on raising standardized test scores. Even candidates who in other areas could draw on broad evidence and deep investigation to inform their politics were settling for the dominant educational frame that was both ill-informed and ideologically driven. So, too, with the candidate who eventually became mayor, Rahm

Emanuel, whose education platform emphasized what individuals (school leaders, teachers, parents, students) could do
differently, rather than systemic reform.

In January 2011 in response to this sorry state of affairs a
large and diverse group of Chicago area educational researchers began assembling to develop a popular curriculum for
educational improvement based on solid research rather than
orthodoxy or ideological dispositions. We started by thinking about the faith-based, fact-free claims that are repeatedly
made about what is wrong with public schools and what will
solve these problems, and realized that our goal should be
to re-articulate the public debates about education—that is,
to push the conversation to address the bigger picture, the
deeper problems that get masked in rhetoric and campaign,
and to foreground evidence. This dynamic moment, a time of
disequilibrium and dislocation, was also an opportunity for
intervention. We wanted to be of use.

We identified four broad visions, fleshed out with recom-
mended actions, pledges for leaders, and resources for further
inquiry in a working document, *Chicago School Reform: Myths,
Realities, and New Visions* (originally published in February
2011, updated in June 2011, and available in its entirety at
http://createchicago.blogspot.com). The four visions: provide
bold leadership that addresses difficult systemic problems
and avoids scapegoating the "usual suspects"; develop and
implement educational policy and reform initiatives that are
primarily research-driven, not market-driven; improve teaching and learning effectiveness by developing standards, curri-
cula, and assessments that are skills-based, not sorting-based;
and ensure the support, dignity, and human and civil rights of
every student.

We recruited at least ten researchers in each area who
were and are available for elaboration and further dialogue
about the accompanying myths and realities, forming the

Chicagoland Researchers and Advocates for Transformative Education (CReATE). Setting the stage was a statement of values concerning public education in a democracy, which emphasizes that schools in a democracy should aim to prepare the next generation to be knowledgeable and informed citizens and residents; to be critical thinkers and creative problem solvers; to be ready to contribute positively to communities and workplaces characterized by diversity; and to be healthy, happy, and able to support the well-being of others with compassion and courage.

Our work does not end with a written statement. In March 2011 we organized a public forum, with over 200 in attendance, where we highlighted both the work of researchers and the work of several organizations (of students, educators, parents, and community members) to advocate for research-based school reform. Our collaborations with organizations have continued and grown, including a research partnership with the Chicago Teachers Union that will extend through the 2011–12 academic year. And of course, we waited for the announcement of the new CEO of Chicago Public Schools, and currently, await a response from new CEO Jean-Claude Brizard to our request for a meeting to share our research and our hopes of working collectively on generative, not punitive, school reform. Our request for working collectively is all the more urgent as Mayor Emanuel suggests directions for school reform that are not necessarily based on evidence, including the current emphasis on making the school day longer, rather than, say, making the school day smarter with more effective use of time.

CReATE is one of our attempts to engage this imminently teachable moment, when no one knows all the answers and we are compelled to improvise with the unfinished, the surprising, and the unforeseen. Let's take up this moment with evidence, dialogue, and hope.

A FRAMEWORK FOR ADVOCACY

Faced with an onslaught of disparaging attacks and problematic reforms, advocates of public education often spend much of our time and energy in defense, reacting to each issue separately and distinctly. Now is the time to pause as we imagine more effective ways to collectivize, collaborate, and build coalition. We need to build a broader movement for educational reform.

Why movement building? Movements are what change ideas, change institutions, change history. Elected leaders can do only so much—they are constrained by the very structures of law-making and political life. And even when they want to do the right thing, they will admit that they often need a movement to push them and protect them in changing the status quo. Movements are what amplify different voices, energize different groups, and interweave different causes. In fact, as argued throughout this book, educational reform cross-sects many other pressing national issues, which means that people concerned about war, or prisons, or welfare, or healthcare, or the environment, or the economy, or human and civil rights, and so on, should all see a link to educational reform. As the movement builds, so does the creation: creation of new imaginative possibilities, new ways of relating, new policies and programs, new alternatives to the every day. Yes, we build movement to change laws and policies, but in the process of building movement we also change how we live, and why, and for what.

There is no recipe book for building movement. Just as teacher preparation should refuse to offer lesson plans or strategies that presumably work for all students in all contexts, so too should advocacy refuse to offer strategies for all to replicate without attention to the particularities of the local context and the strengths of the local actors. But looking to past movements, we can see helpful guides. What follows, then, is a framework that consists of a set of questions that I have found to be useful in assessing our current work and imagining new possibilities. These questions of who, what, when, where, why, and how invite me to tell a story that stands in stark contrast to the stories permeating society today about who is to blame and what constitutes reform.

Who are our allies? Movement building requires mobilizing the public, and this cannot happen unless multiple constituents see this as their issue and invest in change. The Civil Rights Movement had many constituents—religious groups, youth groups, worker groups, neighborhood groups, ally groups, and so on—who sometimes worked together, sometimes worked in parallel, sometimes agreed and sometimes disagreed, but shared a larger vision and a commitment to communicate with and a refusal to be pitted against one another. Public education similarly has multiple constituents, including teachers and other school employees, parents, students, community advocates, taxpayers, researchers, nonprofit and for-profit service providers, politicians and leaders, and really, anyone concerned about our children and our future, and each has unique resources to leverage, from funding to communication networks to access to the decision-making process. Movement building requires forming coalitions with these various constituents in ways that build on their strengths. For example, to point to the lack of research that supports current reforms, and to draw on solid research to propose viable alternatives, have community-based initiatives tapped into local university researchers, and for their part, have local university researchers leveraged their resources to bring research to bear on school reform debates? Citywide networks of researchers, like CReATE in Chicago, are forming in cities across the nation, and constitute one of the newest formations with which to build movement.

What are the problems? I began this book with three questions posed by Lani Guinier that complicate how we think about the problem to be solved. Too often, we ask only the first question, *Who is winning and who is losing,* as if helping the loser to better compete is and should be the primary goal. But particularly in today's context where billionaires are driving school reform, we also need to be asking *Who made the rules* as we try to unravel how reforms are designed to most benefit those who are already winning. Furthermore, at a time when both political parties are proposing reforms that differ very little in intent and outcome, we must be asking questions that help us to question what has become common sense in educational debates that mask the bigger picture and erase dissent, questions like, *What are the stories that we tell the losers to get them to want to continue playing?* Strategic planning that does not begin with these three questions risks defining the problems too narrowly and limiting the possible solutions.

When will we see our goals met? Movements need both short- and long-term goals. One short-term goal might be legislative change. For example, at the time of writing this book, the prospect of a grand overhaul of NCLB looks dim, but change can still happen because Congress has already begun to debate a string of legislation that changes NCLB one component at a time. Such piecemeal revision actually provides fertile ground for forming coalitions, raising public consciousness, and lobbying for change that addresses the various bigger-picture issues raised in this book. The fall of 2011, therefore, offers many opportunities to accomplish short-term goals of minor legislative victories, and scholars and activists have long argued that early minor victories can play a pivotal role in catalyzing mass mobilization and movement building. But movement toward what? The goal of movement building also requires articulating longer-term goals. The Civil Rights Movement provides helpful models for long-term planning, including its decade-long strategy of establishing precedent in lower courts that laid the ground-work for overturning legal segregation by way of the 1954 U.S. Supreme Court case of *Brown v. Board of Education*. In addition to changes in law, longterm goals must also include changes in public consciousness, changes in common sense. In practice, this means that, along with lobbying for policy change, advocates must also engage in media and popular-education campaigns that reframe the debate, expose the bigger picture, and offer alternative visions.

Where should we act? Reframing the debate does not happen by simply creating a catchy tagline. Not only is what we say important, but also how we say it. Who is speaking, to whom, via what media, in what venue, how often, how loudly, how compellingly? My ideas about moving from blaming teachers to seeing the bigger picture do little to change educational debates and policies if I converse only with people who already agree with me. I must also be meeting with partner organizations, facilitating workshops and public forums for various constituent groups, writing articles and speaking in interviews for the news media, blogging on the Internet, issuing press releases and other public statements, lobbying my elected officials, speaking with my own family and former classmates and neighbors, marching with signs in the streets, rallying with bullhorns at the capital, dancing in a flash mob downtown, painting in a public mural in the park, performing with an open mic, and of course, continuing to do my own homework and learning from others in order to resist complicity and self-righteousness. A preliminary step in strategizing any movement building is an assessment or inventory of partners and assets; that is, a mapping of who can do what, including who has access to which audience by what media and with what skill sets and resources. An asset map ensures that we are utilizing our strengths to reach our many constituents.

Why do we need to reframe? This is perhaps the most fundamental of questions to urge our elected officials and educational leaders to ask. I do not wish to demonize the politicians and the investors and the superintendents who are leading the problematic reforms described in this book, because I trust that many of them honestly believe that they are doing what is in the best interest of our nation and of our children. But good intentions do not always lead to good changes. In a context where common sense has been framed by ideologies rooted for decades in efforts to undo public education, we should not be surprised that current reforms are producing the exact opposite of the stated goals, including and especially reforms that come from politicians who identify as liberal, investors who identify as altruistic, and superintendents who identify as proponents of public school teachers and advocates of those students who are struggling the most. Improving public education requires more than having good intentions. It requires more than our common sense. It requires doing our homework.

How do we do all of this? Movement building requires strategic planning. It requires building coalitions and drawing on their strengths, assessing the landscape and drawing on solid research to understand the problems and possible solutions with complexity and nuance, defining short and longterm goals, engaging in multiple initiatives that target changes in not only policy and practice, but also public consciousness, seeing the bigger picture as we question common sense, and laying all of this out in a plan that includes what is to be done, by whom, when, where, how, and with what outcomes, what next steps.

We are not alone. Examples abound of community and nationwide organizing that has successfully redirected educational reform and reclaimed public education. Such examples serve not only as guides and inspirations, but also as evidence that significant change is already happening. Change is inevitable, which means that we can stand by and watch, or we can intervene, engage, innovate, create, transform. Yes, change is inevitable, and therefore, we all have a role to play in ensuring that those changes reflect our vision and our values. Too often, the problems seem overwhelming, and the barriers insurmountable. But our responsibility to our children and our next generation, as members of our communities, as participants in our democracy, is to refuse to lie complacent and complicit. Now is the time to clarify our values, our ideals, our aspirations, our hopes, as we courageously reimagine what our schools can and should look like, and how to get there. Let's build a movement to transform America's schools into places truly deserving of our children.

Notes

Introduction

1. Guinier, L., & Torres, G. (2003). *The miner's canary: Enlisting race, resisting power, transforming democracy.* Cambridge, MA: Harvard University Press.

2. Ladson-Billings, G. (2006). From the achievement gap to the education debt: Understanding achievement in U.S. schools. *Educational Researcher 35*(7), 3–12.

3. Obama, B. (2009, March 10). *Remarks by the President to the Hispanic Chamber of Commerce on a complete and competitive American education.* http://www.whitehouse.gov/the-press-office/remarks-president-united-states-hispanic-chamber-commerce (accessed October 16, 2011).

4. Duncan, A. (2010, July 27). *The quiet revolution: Secretary Arne Duncan's remarks at the National Press Club.* http://www.ed.gov/news/speeches/quiet-revolution-secretary-arne-duncans-remarks-national-press-club (accessed October 16, 2011).

5. Bushaw, W. J., & Lopez, S. J. (2011, September). Betting on teachers: The 43rd annual Phi Delta Kappa/Gallup Poll of the public's attitudes toward the public schools. *Phi Delta Kappan, 93*(1), 8–26.

6. Kopp, W. (2003). *One day, all children . . . : The unlikely triumph of Teach For America and what I learned along the way.* New York: PublicAffairs.

7. Meiners, E. (2007). *Right to be hostile: Schools, prisons, and the making of public enemies.* New York: Routledge.

Chapter 1

1. Tyack, D. B., & Tobin, W. (1994). The "grammar" of schooling: Why has it been so hard to change? *American Educational Research Journal 31*(3), 453–479.

2. Bales, S. N. (2011). Framing education reform: A Frameworks MessageMemo. *Frameworks Institute.* http://www.frameworksinstitute.org (accessed October 15, 2011).

Chapter 2

1. Johnson, C. (2000). *Blowback: The costs and consequences of American empire.* New York: Henry Holt and Company.

2. Berliner, D. C., & Biddle, B. J. (1996). *The manufactured crisis: Myths, fraud, and the attack on America's public schools.* Cambridge, MA: Perseus Books.

3. Lakoff, G. (2004). *Don't think of an elephant: Know your values and frame the debate.* New York: Chelsea Green Publishing.

4. Blount, J. M. (2005). *Fit to teach: Same-sex desire, gender, and school work in the twentieth century.* Albany: State University of New York Press.

5. Apple, M. W. (2006). *Educating the "right" way: Markets, standards, God, and inequality.* New York: Routledge.

6. Woodson, C. G. (2003). *The mis-education of the negro.* San Francisco: Book Tree. (Original work published 1933)

7. Anyon, J. (1979). Ideology and United States history textbooks. *Harvard Educational Review 3,* 361–386; Sadker, M., & Sadker, D. (1994). *Failing at fairness: How our schools cheat girls.* New York: Touchstone.

8. Spring, J. (2009). *Deculturalization and the struggle for equality: A brief history of the education of dominated cultures in the United States.* New York: McGraw-Hill; Tamura, E. H. (1994). *Americanization, acculturation, and ethnic identity: The Nisei generation in Hawaii.* Urbana: University of Illinois Press. Kaomea, J. (2000). A Curriculum of aloha? Colonialism and tourism in Hawai`i's elementary textbooks. *Curriculum Inquiry 30*(3), 319–344.

9. Prashad, V. (2006.) The global war against teachers. *Radical History Review 95,* 9–20.

10. Duggan, L. (2003). *The twilight of equality: Neoliberalism, cultural politics, and the attack on democracy.* Boston: Beacon Press.

11. Klein, N. (2007). *The shock doctrine: The rise of disaster capitalism.* New York: Picador.

12. Weiner, L. (2007). A lethal threat to U.S. teacher education. *Journal of Teacher Education 58*(4), 274–286.

13. Fleming, J., et al. (2009). *Examining CPS' plan to close, phase out, consolidate, turn-around 22 schools.* Chicago: Collaborative for Equity and Justice in Education, University of Illinois at Chicago; Grossman, P., & Loeb, S. (Eds.). (2008). *Alternative routes to teaching: Mapping the new landscape of teacher education.* Cambridge, MA: Harvard University Press.

14. Fuller, B. (2003). Education policy under cultural pluralism. *Educational Researcher 32*(9), 15–24.

Chapter 3

1. Cochran-Smith, M., & Zeichner, K. M. (Eds.). (2005). *Studying teacher education: The report of the AERA panel on research and teacher education.* Mahwah, NJ: Lawrence Erlbaum. Cochran-Smith, M., Feiman-Nemser, S., McIntyre, D. J., & Demers, K. E. (Eds.). (2008). *Handbook of research on teacher education: Enduring questions in changing contexts.* New York: Routledge.

2. Cochran-Smith & Zeichner. *Studying teacher education*; Grossman & Loeb, *Alternative routes.*

3. Kaestle, C. (1983). *Pillars of the republic: Common schools and American society, 1780–1860.* New York: Hill & Wang.

4. Mittal, A., &Gustin, F. (2006). *Turning the tide: Challenging the right on campus.* Oakland, CA: Oakland Institute and Institute for Democratic Education and Culture.

5. Lugg, C. A. (2000). Reading, writing, and reconstruction: The Christian right and the politics of public education. *Educational Policy* 14(5), 622–637; Lugg, C. A. (2001). The Christian right: A cultivated collection of interest groups. *Educational Policy* 15(1), 41–57.

6. Apple, M. W. (2007). Who needs teacher education? Gender technology, and the work of home schooling. *Teacher Education Quarterly* 34(2), 111–130.

7. Imig, D. G., & Imig, S. R. (2008). From traditional certification to competitive certification: A twenty-five year retrospective. In Cochran-Smith, M., et al. (Eds.), *Handbook of research on teacher education: Enduring questions in changing contexts* (pp., 886–907). New York: Routledge.

8. Weiner, A Lethal Threat, 274–286.

9. *World development report 2004: Making services work for poor people.* (2003) http://econ.worldbank.org/wdr/wdr2004/text-30023/ (accessed October 16, 2011).

10. Duncan, A. (2009, October 22). *Teacher preparation: Reforming the uncertain profession—Remarks of Secretary Arne Duncan at Teachers College, Columbia University.* http://www2.ed.gov/news/speeches/2009/10/10222009.html (accessed October 16, 2011).

11. Berlak, A. (2011). Can standardized teacher performance assesment identify highly qualified teachers? In R. Ahlquist et al. (Eds.), *Assault on kids: How hyper-accountability, corporatization, deficit ideologies, and Ruby Payne are destroying our schools* (pp. 51–62). New York: Peter Lang Publishing.

12. Hout, M., & Elliot, S. W. (Eds.). (2011). *Incentives and test-based accountability in education.* Washington, DC: National Academies Press.

Chapter 4

1. Watkins, W. (2001). The White architects of Black education: Ideology and power in America, 1865–1954. New York: Teachers College Press.

2. Mittal & Gustin, *Turning the tide*; Tyack, D. B. (1974). *The one best system: A history of American urban education.* Cambridge, MA: Harvard University Press.

3. DeMarrais, K. (2006). The haves and the have mores: Fueling a conservative ideological war on public education (or tracking the money). *Educational Studies 39*(3), 201–240.

4. Krehely, J., House, M., & Kernan, E. (2004). *Axis of ideology: Conservative foundations and public policy.* Washington, DC: National Committee for Responsive Philanthropy.

5. Hursh, D. (2007). Assessing No Child Left Behind and the rise of neoliberal education policies. *American Education Research Journal 44*(3), 493–518.

6. Saltman, K. (2010). *The gift of education: Public education and venture philanthropy.* New York: Palgrave Macmillan; Scott, J. (2009). The politics of venture philanthropy in charter school policy and advocacy. *Educational Policy 23*(1), 106–136.

7. Lipman, P. (2011). *The new political economy of urban education: Neoliberalism, race, and the right to the city.* New York: Routledge.

8. Fleming et al., *Examining CPS' plan.*

9. Center for Public Integrity. (2011, May 1). Back to school for the billionaires. *Newsweek,* http://www.newsweek.com/2011/05/01/back-to-school-for-the-billionaires.html (accessed October 16, 2011).

Index

About the Author

Kevin K. Kumashiro, Ph.D., is professor of Asian American Studies and education at the University of Illinois at Chicago, where he was formerly chair of the Department of Educational Policy Studies. He has taught in schools and colleges across the United States and abroad, and has served as a consultant for schools, districts, organizations, and agencies. He has authored or edited eight books, including *Troubling Education*, which received the 2003 Gustavus Myers Outstanding Book Award. His more recent books include *Against Common Sense: Teaching and Learning Toward Social Justice*, and *The Seduction of Common Sense: How the Right Has Framed the Debate on America's Schools*. In 2002, he founded the Center for Anti-Oppressive Education, and in 2012, he will become president of the National Association for Multicultural Education.